BASIC DOCUMENTS IN
UNITED STATES
FOREIGN POLICY

THOMAS P. BROCKWAY, 1898-

Dean of Bennington College

AN ANVIL ORIGINAL
under the general editorship of
LOUIS L. SNYDER

D. VAN NOSTRAND COMPANY, INC.
PRINCETON, NEW JERSEY
TORONTO   LONDON
NEW YORK

For Jean

D. VAN NOSTRAND COMPANY, INC.
120 Alexander St., Princeton, New Jersey (*Principal office*); 24 West 40 St., New York, N.Y.
D. VAN NOSTRAND COMPANY (Canada), LTD.
25 Hollinger Rd., Toronto 16, Canada
D. VAN NOSTRAND COMPANY, LTD.
358, Kensington High Street, London, W.14, England

Library of Congress Catalog Card No. 57-12487

PREFACE

DURING much of our history, wrong decisions in foreign policy could be made at only nominal cost; but today we cannot afford errors in the formulation and execution of foreign policy. While the federal government has primary responsibility in this area, the citizen enjoys a degree of remote control which makes his education in world affairs highly important.

This volume is designed for students of whatever age, or whether enrolled in formal courses, associated in study groups, or engaged in solitary self-education. Its aim is to add interest to the study of United States foreign policy, to give greater depth to its understanding, and to provide a partial basis for the evaluation of our international position and policies in the atomic age.

Bennington, Vt.   THOMAS P. BROCKWAY
August, 1957

TABLE OF CONTENTS

— 1 —

SELF-DETERMINATION: THE DECLARATION OF INDEPENDENCE, JULY 4, 1776[1]

The idea that men have a right to a government of their own choosing has outlived the natural rights philosophy which provided Jefferson with a rationale for American independence. The right of self-determination, by whatever name, has profoundly affected American thinking and, perhaps even more, American emotions about events abroad. Its role in the formulation of policy reached a peak under Woodrow Wilson, but it has continued to influence, and sometimes to plague, the policy-makers in Washington.

✓   ✓   ✓

. . . We hold these truths to be self-evident, that all men are created equal, that they are endowed by their Creator with certain unalienable Rights, that among these are Life, Liberty, and the pursuit of Happiness. That, to secure these rights, Governments are instituted among Men, deriving their just Powers from the consent of the governed. That, whenever any form of Government becomes destructive of these ends, it is the Right of the People to alter or to abolish it, and to institute new Government, laying its foundation on such Principles, and organizing its Powers in such form, as to them shall seem most likely to effect their Safety and Happiness. Prudence, indeed, will dictate that Governments long established should not be changed for light and transient causes; and, accordingly, all experience hath shewn, that mankind are more disposed to suffer, while evils are sufferable, than to right themselves by abolishing the forms to which they are ac-

[1] From W. C. Ford, ed., *Journals of the Continental Congress* (Washington, 1906), V, pp. 510-511.

customed. But, when a long train of abuses and usurpations, pursuing invariably the same Object, evinces a
design to reduce them under absolute Despotism, it is their
right, it is their duty, to throw off such Government, and
to provide new Guards for their future Security. . . .

— 2 —

TREATY OF ALLIANCE WITH FRANCE, FEBRUARY 6, 1778 [1]

*Independence having been declared, Congress sent Ben-
jamin Franklin to Paris to seek aid and recognition for the
new nation. The government of Louis XVI was predis-
posed to assist the enemies of Britain, but delayed formal
alliance until Burgoyne's surrender at Saratoga showed
that the colonial cause had a fighting chance. A Treaty of
Amity and Commerce and the Treaty of Alliance given
below were concluded at Paris on February 6, 1778, and
ratified by Congress on May 4 following. The French
alliance was a crucial factor in the winning of independence, but it was not re-activated when France and Great
Britain resumed hostilities in 1793. The treaty was abrogated by Congress in 1798 at the beginning of an undeclared naval war between the United States and France.*

ARTICLE I. If war should break out between France
and Great Britain during the continuance of the present

[1] From W. M. Malloy, ed., *Treaties, Conventions, Interna-
tional Acts, Protocols and Agreements between the United
States of America and other powers, 1776-1909* (2 vols.,
Washington, 1910), I, pp. 479-482.

war between the United States and England, His Majesty and the said United States shall make it a common cause and aid each other mutually with their good offices, their counsels and their forces, according to the exigence of conjunctures, as becomes good and faithful allies.

ARTICLE II. The essential and direct end of the present defensive alliance is to maintain effectually the liberty, sovereignty, and independence absolute and unlimited, of the said United States, as well in matters of government as of commerce. . . .

ARTICLE V. If the United States should think fit to attempt the reduction of the British power, remaining in the northern parts of America, or the islands of Bermudas, those countries or islands, in case of success, shall be confederated with or dependent upon the said United States.

ARTICLE VI. The Most Christian King renounces forever the possession of the islands of Bermudas, as well as of any part of the continent of North America, which before the Treaty of Paris in 1763, or in virtue of that treaty, were acknowledged to belong to the Crown of Great Britain, or to the United States, heretofore called British Colonies, or which are at this time, or have lately been under the power of the King and Crown of Great Britain.

ARTICLE VII. If His Most Christian Majesty shall think proper to attack any of the islands situated in the Gulph of Mexico, or near that Gulph, which are at present under the power of Great Britain, all the said isles, in case of success, shall appertain to the Crown of France.

ARTICLE VIII. Neither of the two parties shall conclude either truce or peace with Great Britain without the formal consent of the other first obtained; and they mutually engage not to lay down their arms until the independence of the United States shall have been formally or tacitly assured by the treaty or treaties that shall terminate the war. . . .

ARTICLE X. The Most Christian King and the United States agree to invite or admit other powers who may have received injuries from England, to make a common cause with them, and to accede to the present alliance . . .

ARTICLE XI. The two parties guarantee mutually from the present time and forever against all other powers, to wit: The United States to His Most Christian Majesty, the present possessions of the Crown of France in America, as well as those which it may acquire by the future treaty of peace: And His Most Christian Majesty guarantees on his part to the United States their liberty, sovereignty and independence, absolute and unlimited . . . and also their possessions, and the additions or conquests that their confederation may obtain during the war. . . .

— 3 —

PRELIMINARY TREATY OF PEACE WITH BRITAIN, NOVEMBER 30, 1782 [1]

The Franco-American victory at Yorktown led swiftly to the resignation of Lord North and the decision of the Rockingham ministry to end the war even at the cost of American independence. Through the summer and fall of 1782 negotiations went on in Paris between Richard Oswald, representing first the Rockingham, then the Shelburne, ministry and two or more of the American peace commissioners, Franklin, John Jay, John Adams, and Henry Laurens. The preliminary treaty became definitive on September 3, 1783 by which time Britain had concluded a treaty with France. In gaining the cession of the entire Northwest and extensive fishing rights, the Americans were abetted by the Earl of Shelburne's interest in a "peace of reconciliation."

✓   ✓   ✓

Whereas reciprocal advantages and mutual convenience are found by experience to form the only permanent
[1] From Malloy, *Treaties, Conventions, etc.,* I, pp. 580-583.

foundation of peace and friendship between States, it is agreed to form the articles of the proposed treaty on such principles of liberal equity and reciprocity, as that partial advantages (those seeds of discord) being excluded, such a beneficial and satisfactory intercourse between the two countries may be established as to promise and secure to both perpetual peace and harmony.

ARTICLE I. His Britannic Majesty acknowledges the said United States, viz., New Hampshire, Massachusetts Bay, Rhode Island and Providence Plantations, Connecticut, New York, New Jersey, Pennsylvania, Delaware, Maryland, Virginia, North Carolina, South Carolina, and Georgia, to be free, sovereign and independent States; that he treats with them as such, and for himself, his heirs and successors, relinquishes all claims to the Government, propriety and territorial rights of the same, and every part thereof. . . .

ARTICLE II. [*Boundaries defined.*]

ARTICLE III. It is agreed that the people of the United States shall continue to enjoy unmolested the right to take fish of every kind on the Grand Bank, and on all the other banks of Newfoundland; also in the Gulph of St. Lawrence, and at all other places in the sea, where the inhabitants of both countries used at any time heretofore to fish; and also that the inhabitants of the United States shall have liberty to take fish of every kind on such part of the coast of Newfoundland as British fishermen shall use, (but not to dry or cure the same on that island); and also on the coasts, bays and creeks of all other of His Britannic Majesty's dominions in America. . . .

ARTICLE IV. It is agreed that creditors on either side shall meet with no lawful impediment to the recovery of the full value in sterling money of all *bona fide* debts heretofore contracted.

ARTICLE V. It is agreed that the Congress shall earnestly recommend to the legislatures of the respective States to provide for the restitution of all estates, rights and properties which have been confiscated, belonging to real British subjects, and also of the estates, rights and properties of persons resident in districts in the possession of His Majesty's arms, and who have not borne arms against the said United States: And that persons of any other description shall have free liberty to go to any part or parts of any of the thirteen United States, and therein to remain twelve months unmolested in their endeavors to obtain the restitution of such of their estates, rights and properties as may have been confiscated. . . . And it is agreed that all persons who have any interest in confiscated lands, either by debts, marriage settlements or otherwise, shall meet with no lawful impediment in the prosecution of their just rights.

ARTICLE VI. That there shall be no future confiscations made, nor any prosecutions commenced against any person or persons for or by reason of the part which he or they may have taken in the present war, and that no person shall, on that account, suffer any future loss or damage, either in his person, liberty or property; and that those who may be in confinement on such charges, at the time of the ratification of the treaty in America, shall be immediately set at liberty, and the prosecutions so commenced be discontinued.

ARTICLE VII. There shall be a firm and perpetual peace between His Britannic Majesty and the said States, and between the subjects of the one and the citizens of the other, wherefore all hostilities, both by sea and land, shall then immediately cease: All prisoners, on both sides, shall be set at liberty; and His Britannic Majesty shall, with all convenient speed, and without causing any destruction, or carrying away any negroes or other property of the American inhabitants, withdraw all his armies, garrisons and fleets from the said United States, and from every port, place and harbour within the same, leaving in all fortifications the American artillery that may be therein. . . .

ARTICLE VIII. The navigation of the river Mississippi, from its source to the ocean, shall forever remain free and open to the subjects of Great Britain and the citizens of the United States. . . .

PROCLAMATION OF NEUTRALITY, APRIL 22, 1793[1]

The French Revolution led swiftly to war on the continent, and early in 1793, following the execution of Louis XVI, France and Great Britain were at war again. The Treaty of Alliance between the United States and France contained no terminal date, and many Americans were warmly partisan to the new French Republic. Washington's cabinet was sharply divided on the French Revolution, but it now unanimously advised against taking sides in the war. The proclamation was framed without benefit of the word "neutrality" in deference to Jefferson's view that the choice of war or neutrality lay with Congress.

◀   ◀   ◀

BY THE PRESIDENT OF THE UNITED STATES OF AMERICA

A PROCLAMATION

Whereas it appears that a state of war exists between Austria, Prussia, Sardinia, Great Britain, and the United Netherlands, on the one part, and France on the other; and the duty and interest of the United States require, that they should with sincerity and good faith adopt and pursue a conduct friendly and impartial towards the belligerent powers:

I have therefore thought fit by these presents, to declare the disposition of the United States to observe the conduct aforesaid towards those powers respectively, and to exhort and warn the citizens of the United States carefully to

[1] From James D. Richardson, ed., *Messages and Papers of the Presidents, 1789-1905* (Washington, 1907) I, pp. 156-157.

avoid all acts and proceedings whatsoever which may in any manner tend to contravene such disposition.

And I do hereby also make known that whosoever of the citizens of the United States shall render himself liable to punishment or forfeiture under the law of nations by committing, aiding, or abetting hostilities against any of the said powers, or by carrying to any of them those articles which are deemed contraband by the modern usage of nations, will not receive the protection of the United States against such punishment or forfeiture; and further, that I have given instructions to those officers to whom it belongs, to cause prosecutions to be instituted against all persons who shall, within the cognizance of the courts of the United States, violate the law of nations with respect to the powers at war, or any of them.

In testimony whereof I have caused the seal of the United States of America to be affixed to these presents, and signed the same with my hand.

Done at the city of Philadelphia, the 22nd day of April, 1793, and of the Independence of the United States of America the seventeenth.

Go. Washington

Th. Jefferson

— 5 —

FIRST NEUTRALITY ACT, JUNE 5, 1794[1]

Washington's proclamation of neutrality failed to restrain Citizen Edmond Genêt, minister of the French Republic, who arrived at Charleston in April, 1793 and at once made the United States a base of elaborate oper-

[1] From *Acts passed at the Third Congress of the United States of America* (Philadelphia, 1794), pp. 97-102.

*ations against both Britain and Spain. In August the gov-
ernment requested Genêt's recall and rather belatedly published a list of rules for giving effect to its policy of
neutrality. In the following year Congress passed the first
neutrality act in American history for the purpose of
declaring illegal everything Genêt had done, and pre-
scribing penalties for future offenders. In a sense a testi-
monial to Genêt, this act is a remarkable statement of
the obligations of a neutral.*

✓   ✓   ✓

Section 1. Be it enacted and declared by the Senate
and House of Representatives of the United States, in
Congress assembled,

That if any citizen of the United States shall within
the territory or jurisdiction of the same accept and exercise a commission to serve a foreign prince or state in
war by land or sea the person so offending shall be
deemed guilty of a high misdemeanor and shall be fined
not more than two thousand dollars and shall be imprisoned not exceeding three years.

Section 2. And be it further enacted and declared,
that if any person shall within the territory or jurisdiction
of the United States enlist or enter himself, or hire or
retain another person to enlist or enter himself, or to go
beyond the limits or jurisdiction of the United States with
intent to be enlisted or entered in the service of any foreign prince or state as a soldier, or as a marine or seaman
on board of any vessel of war, letter of marque or priva-
teer, every person so offending shall be deemed guilty of
a high misdemeanor and shall be fined not exceeding one
thousand dollars, and be imprisoned not exceeding three
years. . . .

Section 3. And be it further enacted and declared,
That if any person shall within any of the ports, harbors,
bays, rivers or other waters of the United States, fit out
and arm or attempt to fit out and arm, or procure to be
fitted out and armed, or shall knowingly be concerned
in the furnishing, fitting out or arming of any ship or
vessel with intent that such ship or vessel shall be employed in the service of any foreign prince or state to
cruise or commit hostilities upon the subjects, citizens,
or property of another foreign prince or state with whom

the United States are at peace, or shall issue or deliver a commission within the territory or jurisdiction of the United States for any ship or vessel to the intent that she may be employed as aforesaid, every such person so offending shall upon conviction be adjudged guilty of a high misdemeanor and shall be fined and imprisoned at the discretion of the court in which the conviction shall be had, so as the fine to be imposed shall in no case be more than five thousand dollars and the term of imprisonment shall not exceed three years . . .

Section 4. And be it further enacted, and declared, That if any person shall within the territory or jurisdiction of the United States encrease or augment or procure to be encreased or augmented or shall be knowingly concerned in encreasing or augmenting the force of any ship of war, cruiser or other armed vessel which at the time of her arrival within the United States, was a ship of war, cruiser or armed vessel in the service of a foreign prince or state or belonging to the subjects or citizens of such prince or state the same being at war with another foreign prince or state with whom the United States are at peace, by adding to the number or size of the guns of such vessel prepared for use, or by the addition thereto of any equipment solely applicable to war, every such person so offending shall upon conviction be adjudged guilty of a misdemeanor and shall be fined and imprisoned at the discretion of the court in which the conviction shall be had, so as that such fine shall not exceed one thousand dollars nor the term of imprisonment be more than one year.

Section 5. And be it further enacted and declared, That if any person shall within the territory or jurisdiction of the United States begin or set on foot or provide or prepare the means for any military expedition or enterprize to be carried on from thence against the territory or dominions of any foreign prince or state with whom the United States are at peace, every such person so offending shall upon conviction be adjudged guilty of a high misdemeanor and shall suffer fine and imprisonment at the discretion of the court in which the conviction shall be had, so as that such fine shall not exceed three thousand dollars nor the term of imprisonment be more than three years. . . .

— 6 —

WASHINGTON'S FAREWELL ADDRESS, SEPTEMBER 17, 1796[1]

Washington timed his famous valedictory to stifle any thought that he might be persuaded to serve as President for a third term, but his main concern was to publish his views and advice on statecraft and policy as "the disinterested warnings of a parting friend." His emphatic advice against involvement in European politics has long served the proponents of American isolationism, but Washington himself looked upon neutrality not as an absolute good, but as an essential condition of the young republic's growth to strength and maturity. The Farewell Address is read in the two houses of Congress on February 22 of each year.

Friends and Fellow-Citizens:

. . . Observe good faith and justice toward all nations. Cultivate peace and harmony with all. Religion and morality enjoin this conduct. And can it be that good policy does not equally enjoin it? It will be worthy of a free, enlightened, and at no distant period a great nation to give to mankind the magnanimous and too novel example of a people always guided by an exalted justice and benevolence. . . .

In the execution of such a plan nothing is more essential than that permanent, inveterate antipathies against particular nations and passionate attachments for others should be excluded, and that in place of them just and amicable feelings toward all should be cultivated. . . . Antipathy

[1] From Richardson, ed., *Messages and Papers of the Presidents*, I, pp. 213-224.

in one nation against another disposes each more readily to offer insult and injury, to lay hold of slight causes of umbrage, and to be haughty and intractable when accidental or trifling occasions of dispute occur.

Hence frequent collisions, obstinate, envenomed, and bloody contests. The nation prompted by ill will and resentment sometimes impels to war the government contrary to the best calculations of policy. . . .

So, likewise, a passionate attachment of one nation for another produces a variety of evils. Sympathy for the favorite nation, facilitating the illusion of an imaginary common interest in cases where no real common interest exists, and infusing into one the enmities of the other, betrays the former into a participation in the quarrels and wars of the latter without adequate inducement or justification. It leads also to concessions to the favorite nation of privileges denied to others, . . . and it gives to ambitious, corrupted, or deluded citizens (who devote themselves to the favorite nation) facility to betray or sacrifice the interests of their own country without odium, sometimes even with popularity. . . .

Against the insidious wiles of foreign influence (I conjure you to believe me, fellow-citizens) the jealousy of a free people ought to be *constantly* awake, since history and experience prove that foreign influence is one of the most baneful foes of republican government. But that jealousy, to be useful, must be impartial, else it becomes the instrument of the very influence to be avoided, instead of a defense against it. . . .

The great rule of conduct for us in regard to foreign nations is, in extending our commercial relations to have with them as little *political* connection as possible. So far as we have already formed engagements let them be fulfilled with perfect good faith. Here let us stop.

Europe has a set of primary interests which to us have none or a very remote relation. Hence she must be engaged in frequent controversies, the causes of which are essentially foreign to our concerns. Hence, therefore, it must be unwise in us to implicate ourselves by artificial ties in the ordinary vicissitudes of her politics or the ordinary combinations and collisions of her friendships or enmities.

Our detached and distant situation invites and enables

us to pursue a different course. If we remain one people, under an efficient government, the period is not far off when we may defy material injury from external annoyance; when we may take such an attitude as will cause the neutrality we may at any time resolve upon to be scrupulously respected; when belligerent nations, under the impossibility of making acquisitions upon us, will not lightly hazard the giving us provocation; when we may choose peace or war, as our interest, guided by justice, shall counsel.

Why forego the advantages of so peculiar a situation? Why quit our own to stand upon foreign ground? Why, by interweaving our destiny with that of any part of Europe, entangle our peace and prosperity in the toils of European ambition, rivalship, interest, humor, or caprice?

It is our true policy to steer clear of permanent alliances with any portion of the foreign world, so far, I mean, as we are now at liberty to do it; for let me not be understood as capable of patronizing infidelity to existing engagements. . . .

Taking care always to keep ourselves by suitable establishments on a respectable defensive posture, we may safely trust to temporary alliances for extraordinary emergencies. . . .

In relation to the still subsisting war in Europe my proclamation [*of neutrality*] of the 22d of April, 1793, is the index to my plan. . . .

After deliberate examination, with the aid of the best lights I could obtain, I was well satisfied that our country, under all the circumstances of the case, had a right to take, and was bound in duty and interest to take, a neutral position. Having taken it, I determined as far as should depend upon me to maintain it with moderation, perseverance, and firmness. . . .

The inducements of interest for observing that conduct will best be referred to your own reflections and experience. With me a predominant motive has been to endeavor to gain time to our country to settle and mature its yet recent institutions, and to progress without interruption to that degree of strength and consistency which is necessary to give it, humanly speaking, the command of its own fortunes. . . .

CESSION OF LOUISIANA, APRIL 30, 1803[1]

Late in 1800 Napoleon extorted the immense territory of Louisiana from Spain, and the prospect of French power established at New Orleans led Jefferson to conclude that we would have to "marry ourselves to the British fleet and nation." But it was possible that Napoleon would yield control of the Mississippi by selling New Orleans, and James Monroe was sent to Paris to find out. Fortunately for his mission, Napoleon, exasperated by French losses to rebellion and disease in Santo Domingo, had just determined to give up empire-building in the New World. After some haggling, Monroe and Robert Livingston, the American minister to France, agreed to pay $15,000,000 of which $3,750,000 would meet the claims of American citizens against France for losses at sea. Jefferson had grave doubt about the constitutionality of the purchase, but this did not deter him, and the treaty was overwhelmingly approved by the Senate. The Supreme Court later upheld the right of the United States to acquire and govern new territory and to confer statehood on it and citizenship on its inhabitants.

⚊⚊⚊

Treaty for the Cession of Louisiana

ARTICLE I. Whereas, by the Article the third of the Treaty concluded at St. Idelfonso (*sic*) the 1st October 1800 between the First Consul of the French Republic and his Catholic Majesty it was agreed as follows—"His Catholic Majesty promises and engages on his part to cede the French Republic six months after the full and entire execution of the conditions and stipulations herein relative

[1] From Malloy, *Treaties, Conventions, etc.*, I, pp. 508-516.

to his Royal Highness the Duke of Parma, the Colony or Province of Louisiana with the same extent that it now has in the hands of Spain, and that it had when France possessed it; and such as it should be after the Treaties subsequently entered into between Spain and other States."

And whereas in pursuance of the Treaty and particularly of the third article the French Republic has an incontestible title to the domain and to the possession of the said Territory—the First Consul of the French Republic desiring to give to the United States a strong proof of his friendship doth hereby cede to the said United States in the name of the French Republic forever and in full sovereignty the said territory with all its rights and appurtenances. . . .

ARTICLE III. The inhabitants of the ceded territory shall be incorporated in the Union of the United States and admitted as soon as possible according to the principles of the Federal Constitution to the enjoyment of all the rights, advantages and immunities of citizens of the United States; and in the mean time they shall be maintained and protected in the free enjoyment of their liberty, property and the Religion which they profess. . . .

ARTICLE V. Immediately after the ratification of the present Treaty . . . the Commissary of the French Republic shall remit all military posts of New Orleans and other parts of the ceded territory to the Commissary or Commissaries named by the President to take possession. . . .

ARTICLE VI. The United States promise to execute such treaties and articles as may have been agreed between Spain and the tribes and nations of Indians until by mutual consent of the United States and the said tribes or nations other suitable articles shall have been agreed upon. . . .

Done at Paris the 30th of April 1803.

ROBERT R. LIVINGSTON
JAMES MONROE
BARBÉ MARBOIS

— 8 —

THE EMBARGO ACT, DECEMBER 22, 1807 [1]

Napoleon's "Continental System" and Britain's block-ade of France and her satellites placed American shipping in double jeopardy. Jefferson was unwilling to risk war, but he thought the belligerents might be persuaded to respect American rights at sea by economic pressures. On December 18, 1807 he invited Congress to consider the possibility of ordering American merchant ships to remain in port for their own safety. Congress wasted no time in passing a sweeping embargo act which protected infant industries, encouraged smuggling, injured American ship-ping interests, and had no visible effect on the behavior of the warring powers. The Embargo Act gave way in fifteen months to the less drastic, but equally ineffective Non-Intercourse Act which was repealed in 1810.

✓   ✓   ✓

An Act laying an Embargo on all ships and vessels in the ports and harbors of the United States.

Be it enacted by the Senate and House of Representa-tives of the United States of America in Congress as-sembled, That an embargo be, and hereby is laid on all ships and vessels in the ports and places within the limits or jurisdiction of the United States, cleared or not cleared, bound to any foreign port or place; and that no clearance be furnished to any ship or vessel bound to such foreign port or place, except vessels under the immediate direc-tion of the President of the United States. . . .

Section 2. And be it further enacted, That during the continuance of this act, no registered, or sea letter vessel,

[1] From Richard Peters, ed., *The Public Statutes at Large of the United States of America* (Boston, 1854), II, pp. 451-453.

having on board goods, wares and merchandise, shall be
allowed to depart from one port of the United States to
any other within the same, unless the master, owner, con-
signee or factor of such vessel shall first give bond, with
one or more sureties to the collector of the district from
which she is bound to depart, in a sum of double the
value of the vessel and cargo, that the said goods, wares,
or merchandise shall be relanded in some port of the
United States, dangers of the sea excepted, which bond,
and also a certificate from the collector where the same
may be relanded, shall by the collector respectively be
transmitted to the Secretary of the Treasury. All armed
vessels possessing public commissions from any foreign
power, are not to be considered as liable to the embargo
as laid by this act.

— 9 —

MADISON'S WAR MESSAGE,
JUNE 1, 1812[1]

*During the Napoleonic wars, the United States had
concrete grievances against France as well as against
Great Britain for interference with neutral shipping and
trade, and a Senate motion to include France in the
declaration of war against Britain lost by a narrow mar-
gin. But France had not "impressed" American seamen,
and the British were held responsible for the remarkable
confederacy that Tecumseh had formed to stop the west-
ward advance of settlement. Moreover the "war hawks"
were excited by the prospect of wresting Canada from
England and Florida from her impotent ally, Spain. With*

[1] From Richardson, ed., *Messages and Papers of the Presidents,* I, pp. 499-505.

substantial opposition in both houses, Congress voted for war on June 18 two days after Lord Castlereagh had announced that the offending orders-in-council were being repealed.

✓   ✓   ✓

To the Senate and House of Representatives of the United States:

I communicate to Congress certain documents, being a continuation of those heretofore laid before them on the subject of our affairs with Great Britain.

Without going back beyond the renewal in 1803 of the war in which Great Britain is engaged, and omitting unrepaired wrongs of inferior magnitude, the conduct of her Government presents a series of acts hostile to the United States as an independent and neutral nation.

British cruisers have been in the continued practice of violating the American flag on the great highway of nations, and of seizing and carrying off persons sailing under it. . . . Thousands of American citizens, under the safeguard of public law and of their national flag, have been torn from their country and from everything dear to them; have been dragged on board ships of war of a foreign nation ˊand exposed, under the severities of their discipline . . . to risk their lives in the battles of their oppressors. . . .

British cruisers have been in the practice also of violating the rights and the peace of our coasts . . . and have wantonly spilt American blood within the sanctuary of our territorial jurisdiction. . . .

Under pretended blockades, without the presence of an adequate force and sometimes without the practicability of applying one, our commerce has been plundered in every sea, the great staples of our country have been cut off from their legitimate markets. . . .

Not content with these occasional expedients for laying waste our neutral trade, the cabinet of Britain resorted at length to the sweeping system of blockades, under the name of orders in council, which has been molded and managed as might best suit its political views, its commercial jealousies, or the avidity of British cruisers. . . .

It has become, indeed, sufficiently certain that the commerce of the United States is to be sacrificed, not as interfering with the belligerent rights of Great Britain; not as supplying the wants of her enemies, which she herself supplies; but as interfering with the monopoly which she covets for her own commerce and navigation. . . .

In reviewing the conduct of Great Britain toward the United States our attention is necessarily drawn to the warfare just renewed by the savages on one of our extensive frontiers—a warfare which is known to spare neither age nor sex and to be distinguished by features peculiarly shocking to humanity. It is difficult to account for the activity and combinations which have for some time been developing themselves among tribes in constant intercourse with British traders and garrisons without connecting their hostility with that influence and without recollecting the authenticated examples of such interpositions heretofore furnished by the officers and agents of that Government.

Such is the spectacle of injuries and indignities which have been heaped on our country, and such the crisis which its unexampled forbearance and conciliatory efforts have not been able to avert. . . .

Whether the United States shall continue passive under these progressive usurpations and these accumulating wrongs, or, opposing force to force in defense of their national rights, shall commit a just cause into the hands of the Almighty Disposer of Events, avoiding all connections which might entangle it in the contest or views of other powers, and preserving a constant readiness to concur in an honorable reestablishment of peace and friendship, is a solemn question which the Constitution wisely confides to the legislative department of the Government. In recommending it to their early deliberations I am happy in the assurance that the decision will be worthy the enlightened and patriotic councils of a virtuous, a free, and a powerful nation. . . .

DISARMAMENT ON THE GREAT LAKES, APRIL 28, 1818 [1]

Following the War of 1812, the costs and risks of naval rivalry on the Great Lakes prompted an American proposal of disarmament that had been made before and rejected by London. The British government was now agreeable, and an accord was effected through an exchange of letters between Richard Rush, Acting Secretary of State, and Charles Bagot, the British Minister in Washington, in April, 1817. Approval by the Senate a year later gave the accord the status of a treaty and it was published as a presidential proclamation on April 28, 1818. This Rush-Bagot Agreement related only to naval armaments, but it was a milestone on the way to an unguarded frontier between Canada and the United States, and it has remained in effect to the present.

✓   ✓   ✓

A PROCLAMATION

Whereas, an arrangement was entered into . . . between Richard Rush, esquire, at that time acting as Secretary for the Department of State of the United States, for and in behalf of the government of the United States, and the Right Honorable Charles Bagot, His Britannic Majesty's Envoy Extraordinary and Minister Plenipotentiary, for and in behalf of His Britannic Majesty, which arrangement is in the words following, to wit:

"The naval force to be maintained upon the American lakes by His Majesty and the Government of the United States shall henceforth be confined to the following vessels on each side, that is—

[1] From Malloy, *Treaties, Conventions, etc.*, I, p. 630.

"On Lake Ontario, to one vessel not exceeding one hundred tons burden, and armed with one eighteen pound cannon.

"On the Upper Lakes, to two vessels not exceeding like burden each, and armed with like force.

"On the waters of Lake Champlain, to one vessel not exceeding like burden, and armed with like force.

"All other armed vessels on these lakes shall be forthwith dismantled, and no other vessels of war shall be there built or armed.

"If either party should be hereafter desirous of annulling this stipulation, and should give notice to that effect to the other party, it shall cease to be binding after the expiration of six months from the date of such notice.

"The naval force so to be limited shall be restricted to such services as will, in no respect, interfere with the proper duties of the armed vessels of the other party."

And whereas the Senate of the United States have approved of the said arrangement, and recommended that it should be carried into effect, the same having also received the sanction of His Royal Highness the Prince Regent, acting in the name and on behalf of His Britannic Majesty (George III),

Now, therefore, I, James Monroe, President of the United States do, by this my proclamation, make known and declare that the arrangement aforesaid, and every stipulation thereof, has been duly entered into, concluded and confirmed, and is of full force and effect. . . .

By the President
JAMES MONROE

JOHN QUINCY ADAMS,
Secretary of State

THE MONROE DOCTRINE,
DECEMBER 2, 1823[1]

*The bold idea that the American continents were no
longer open to European colonization originated with
Monroe's Secretary of State, John Quincy Adams, who
stated it as policy in a warning to the Russian government in July, 1823. Monroe's warning against European
intervention to restore Spain's rule over her lost colonies
owes much to British initiative. When such intervention
seemed imminent, George Canning, British foreign secretary, proposed an Anglo-American statement that would
signify "our joint disapprobation." Seeking advice, Monroe found Jefferson and Madison warmly disposed toward
Canning's proposal. Its acceptance, Jefferson thought,
would detach Britain from the other powers and bring
"her mighty weight into the scale of free government and
emancipate a continent at one stroke." But Adams
vehemently objected to the United States going along with
Britain "like a cockboat in the wake of the British man-
of-war" and insisted that we make our own statement.
Monroe followed Adams' advice, but removed the pronouncement from diplomatic channels by embodying it in
his Annual Message to Congress. British policy and sea
power then and for some time thereafter filled the gap
between American professions and the means of their enforcement.*

✓   ✓   ✓

Fellow-Citizens of the Senate and House of Representatives:
. . . At the proposal of the Russian Imperial Government, made through the minister of the Emperor residing

[1] From Richardson, *Messages and Papers of the Presidents,*
    II, pp. 207-220.

here, a full power and instructions have been transmitted to the minister of the United States at St. Petersburg to arrange by amicable negotiation the respective rights and interests of the two nations on the northwest coast of this continent. . . . The Government of the United States has been desirous by this friendly proceeding of manifesting the great value which they have invariably attached to the friendship of the Emperor and their solicitude to cultivate the best understanding with his Government. In the discussions to which this interest has given rise and in the arrangements by which they may terminate the occasion has been judged proper for asserting, as a principle in which the rights and interests of the United States are involved, that the American continents, by the free and independent condition which they have assumed and maintain, are henceforth not to be considered as subjects for future colonization by any European powers. . . .

It was stated at the commencement of the last session that a great effort was then making in Spain and Portugal to improve the condition of the people of those countries, and that it appeared to be conducted with extraordinary moderation. It need scarcely be remarked that the result has been so far very different from what was then anticipated. Of events in that quarter of the globe, with which we have so much intercourse and from which we derive our origin, we have always been anxious and interested spectators. The citizens of the United States cherish sentiments the most friendly in favor of the liberty and happiness of their fellow-men on that side of the Atlantic. In the wars of the European powers in matters relating to themselves we have never taken any part, nor does it comport with our policy so to do. It is only when our rights are invaded or seriously menaced that we resent injuries or make preparations for our defense. With the movements in this hemisphere we are of necessity more immediately connected, and by causes which must be obvious to all enlightened and impartial observers. The political system of the allied powers is essentially different in this respect from that of America. . . . We owe it, therefore, to candor and to the amicable relations existing between the United States and those powers to declare that we should consider an attempt on their part to extend their system to any portion of this hemisphere as dangerous to our peace and safety. With the existing colonies or dependencies of any European power we have not interfered and shall not interfere. But with the Governments who have declared their independence and maintained it, and whose independence we have, on great consideration and on just principles, acknowledged, we could not view any interposition for the purpose of oppressing them, or controlling in any other manner their destiny, by any European power in any other light than as the manifestation of an unfriendly disposition toward the United States. . . .

— 12 —

POLK'S DEFENSE OF THE MEXICAN WAR, DECEMBER 8, 1846[1]

President Polk devised several means of realizing his ambition to add California to the Union. First he sent John Slidell to Mexico to offer as much as $25,000,000 for California and New Mexico, but the Mexican government refused to receive the envoy. By this time Polk had sent word to influential Californians that if they were to revolt from Mexico, in the pattern of Texas, the United States would welcome them into the Union. Before the outcome of these two moves was known, the President sent an army under General Taylor into the territory between the Nueces and Rio Grande rivers, which was claimed by both Mexico and Texas, and where a clash of arms might easily lead to war. Finally Polk came to the

[1] From Richardson, ed., *Messages and Papers of the Presidents*, IV, pp. 471-506.

conclusion that Mexico's refusal to pay the accumulated claims of American citizens and her spurning of Slidell provided sufficient grounds for war. After deciding to ask Congress to declare war, Polk learned that Mexican cavalry had killed or wounded sixteen American dragoons in the disputed area. This event, described as the shedding of American blood on American soil, gave Polk's war message its emotional charge, and Congress voted overwhelmingly for war. But the Whigs, including Lincoln, and anti-slavery forces challenged Polk's case for war. Nettled by the criticism, and influenced by the high value Americans set on self-defense, Polk devoted nearly 10,000 words to the "war guilt" question in his Annual Message, seven months after the declaration of war.

✓   ✓   ✓

Fellow-Citizens of the Senate and of the House of Representatives:

. . . The existing war with Mexico was neither desired nor provoked by the United States. On the contrary, all honorable means were resorted to to avert it. After years of endurance of aggravated and unredressed wrongs on our part, Mexico, in violation of solemn treaty stipulations and of every principle of justice recognized by civilized nations, commenced hostilities, and thus by her own act forced the war upon us. Long before the advance of our Army to the left bank of the Rio Grande we had ample cause of war against Mexico, and had the United States resorted to this extremity we might have appealed to the whole civilized world for the justice of our cause. I deem it to be my duty to present to you on the present occasion a condensed review of the injuries we had sustained, of the causes which led to the war, and of its progress since its commencement. This is rendered the more necessary because of the misapprehensions which have to some extent prevailed as to its origin and true character. The war has been represented as unjust and unnecessary and as one of aggression on our part upon a weak and injured enemy. Such erroneous views, though entertained by but few, have been widely and extensively circulated, not only at home, but have been spread throughout Mexico and the whole world. . . .

The wrongs which we have suffered from Mexico almost ever since she became an independent power and the patient endurance with which we have borne them are without parallel in the history of modern civilized nations. . . .

Scarcely had Mexico achieved her independence, which the United States were the first among the nations to acknowledge, when she commenced the system of insult and spoliation which she has ever since pursued. Our citizens engaged in lawful commerce were imprisoned, their vessels seized, and our flag insulted in her ports. If money was wanted, the lawless seizure and confiscation of our merchant vessels and their cargoes was a ready resource, and if to accomplish their purposes it became necessary to imprison the owners, captains, and crews, it was done. Rulers superseded rulers in Mexico in rapid succession, but still there was no change in this system of depredation. The Government of the United States made repeated reclamations on behalf of its citizens, but these were answered by the perpetration of new outrages. Promises of redress made by Mexico in the most solemn forms were postponed or evaded. . . .

Such are the grave causes of complaint on the part of the United States against Mexico—causes which existed long before the annexation of Texas to the American Union; and yet, animated by the love of peace and a magnanimous moderation, we did not adopt those measures of redress which under such circumstances are the justified resort of injured nations.

The annexation of Texas to the United States constituted no just cause of offense to Mexico. The pretext that it did so is wholly inconsistent and irreconcilable with well-authenticated facts connected with the revolution by which Texas became independent of Mexico. . . .

Texas had been an independent state, with an organized government, defying the power of Mexico to overthrow or reconquer her, for more than ten years before Mexico commenced the present war against the United States. . . . Texas at the period of her annexation to the United States bore the same relation to Mexico that Mexico had borne to Spain for many years before Spain acknowledged her independence, with this important difference, that before the annexation of Texas to the United States was consummated Mexico herself, by a formal act of her Government, had acknowledged the independence of Texas as a nation. . . .

But there are those who, conceding all this to be true, assume the ground that the true western boundary of Texas is the Nueces instead of the Rio Grande, and that therefore in marching our Army to the east bank of the latter river we passed the Texan line and invaded the territory of Mexico. A simple statement of facts known to exist will conclusively refute such an assumption. . . .

The Texas which was ceded to Spain by the Florida treaty of 1819 embraced all the country now claimed by the State of Texas between the Nueces and the Rio Grande. The Republic of Texas always claimed this river as her western boundary, and in her treaty made with Santa Anna in May, 1836, he recognized it as such. By the constitution which Texas adopted in March, 1836, senatorial and representative districts were organized extending west of the Neuces. The Congress of Texas on the 19th of December, 1836, passed "An Act to define the boundaries of the Republic of Texas," in which they declared the Rio Grande from its mouth to its source to be their boundary, and by the said act they extended their "civil and political jurisdiction" over the country up to that boundary. . . .

But Mexico herself has never placed the war which she has waged upon the ground that our Army occupied the intermediate territory between the Nueces and the Rio Grande. Her refuted pretension that Texas was not in fact an independent state, but a rebellious province, was obstinately persevered in, and her avowed purpose in commencing a war with the United States was to reconquer Texas and to restore Mexican authority over the whole territory—not to the Nueces only, but to the Sabine. In view of the proclaimed menaces of Mexico to this effect, I deemed it my duty, as a measure of precaution and defense, to order our Army to occupy a position on our frontier as a military post, from which our troops could best resist and repel any attempted invasion which Mexico might make. . . .

The movement of our Army to the Rio Grande was made by the commanding general under positive orders to abstain from all aggressive acts toward Mexico or Mexican citizens, and to regard the relations between the two countries as peaceful unless Mexico should declare war or commit acts of hostility indicative of a state of war, and these orders he faithfully executed. Whilst occupying his position on the east bank of the Rio Grande, within the limits of Texas, then recently admitted as one of the States of our Union, the commanding general of the Mexican forces, who, in pursuance of the orders of his Government, had collected a large army on the opposite shore of the Rio Grande, crossed the river, invaded our territory, and commenced hostilities by attacking our forces. Thus, after all the injuries which we had received and borne from Mexico, and after she had insultingly rejected a minister sent to her on a mission of peace, and whom she had solemnly agreed to receive, she consummated her long course of outrage against our country by commencing an offensive war and shedding the blood of our citizens on our own soil. . . .

— 13 —

CLAYTON-BULWER TREATY, APRIL 19, 1850[1]

In the 1840's British and American representatives in Central America vigorously competed for inter-oceanic canal routes and rights. American diplomacy secured the United States special transit rights across the Panama Isthmus and exclusive rights to build a canal or railway across Nicaragua. The value of the Nicaragua route depended on control of the San Juan River and of Greytown at its mouth. When the British included Greytown in an existing protectorate and offered to back Costa Rica's claims to part of the San Juan River, tension de-

[1] Malloy, *Treaties, Conventions, etc.*, I, pp. 659-663.

veloped. However, both London and Washington were prepared to compromise and a treaty was drawn up by Taylor's Secretary of State, John M. Clayton, and the British Minister, Sir Henry Bulwer. In view of Britain's dominant sea power in the Caribbean, the United States could not have made good an exclusive claim to canal-building under the Monroe Doctrine, and came off well with an equal partnership. The treaty has a distinctly international tone both in inviting others to join in similar stipulations and in insisting on the neutrality of any canal that might be built. The treaty was superseded in 1901 by the Hay-Pauncefote Treaty.

ARTICLE I. The Governments of the United States and Great Britain hereby declare that neither the one nor the other will ever obtain or maintain for itself any exclusive control over the (Nicaragua) ship-canal; agreeing that neither will ever erect or maintain any fortifications commanding the same, or in the vicinity thereof, or occupy, or fortify, or colonize, or assume or exercise any dominion over Nicaragua, Costa Rica, the Mosquito coast, or any part of Central America. . . .

ARTICLE II. Vessels of the United States or Great Britain traversing the said canal shall, in case of war between the contracting parties, be exempted from blockade, detention, or capture by either of the belligerents; and this provision shall extend to such distance from the two ends of the said canal as may hereafter be found expedient to establish.

ARTICLE III. In order to secure the construction of the said canal, the contracting parties engage that, if any such canal shall be undertaken upon fair and equitable terms by any parties having the authority of the local government or governments through whose territory the same may pass, then the persons employed in making the said canal, and their property used or to be used for that object, shall be protected, from the commencement of the said canal to its completion, by the United States and Great Britain, from unjust detention, confiscation, seizure or any violence whatsoever.

ARTICLE IV. The contracting parties will use whatever influence they respectively exercise with any State,

States or Governments possessing, or claiming to possess, any jurisdiction or right over the territory which the said canal shall traverse . . . in order to induce such States or Governments to facilitate the construction of the said canal by every means in their power. . . .

ARTICLE V. The contracting parties further engage that when the said canal shall have been completed they will protect it from interruption, seizure, or unjust confiscation, and that they will guarantee the neutrality thereof, so that the said canal may forever be open and free, and the capital invested therein secure. . . .

ARTICLE VI. The contracting parties in this convention engage to invite every State with which both or either have friendly intercourse to enter into stipulations with them similar to those which they have entered into with each other, to the end that all other States may share in the honor and advantage of having contributed to a work of such general interest and importance as the canal herein contemplated. . . .

ARTICLE VII. It being desirable that no time should be unnecessarily lost in commencing and constructing the said canal, the United States and Great Britain determine to give their support and encouragement to such persons or company as may first offer to commence the same, with the necessary capital, the consent of the local authorities, and on such principles as accord with the spirit and intention of this convention. . . .

ARTICLE VIII. The United States and Great Britain having not only desired, in entering into this convention, to accomplish a particular object, but also to establish a general principle, they hereby agree to extend their protection, by treaty stipulations, to any other practicable communications, whether by canal or railway, across the isthmus which connects North and South America, and especially to the interoceanic communications, should the same prove to be practicable, whether by canal or railway, which are now proposed to be established by the way of Tehuantepec or Panama. . . .

ON REVOLUTIONS ABROAD:
WEBSTER TO HÜLSEMANN,
DECEMBER 21, 1850[1]

The revolutions that shook Europe in 1848 had an excellent press in the United States, and as reaction triumphed in Germany and Austria, Americans warmly acclaimed Hungary's revolt against the House of Hapsburg, and the establishment in 1849 of the short-lived Hungarian Republic. Riding this wave, President Zachary Taylor decided "to be the first to welcome independent Hungary into the family of nations," and empowered an agent in Europe to offer recognition if circumstances were favorable. But Russian troops, sent to the aid of Austria, defeated the Magyars and their Republic collapsed. A protest against the United States government's avowed interest in Hungary's liberation was lodged with the State Department by Chevalier J. G. Hülsemann, chargé d'affaires *at the Austrian Legation. Webster's boastful reply made it clear that the American government would continue to cheer on the forces of liberalism abroad, but would do nothing to give weight to its words or the words of the American people.*

✓　　　✓　　　✓

. . . The power of this republic, at the present moment, is spread over a region one of the richest and most fertile on the globe, and of an extent in comparison with which the possessions of the House of Hapsburg are but as a patch on the earth's surface. Its population, already twenty-five millions, will exceed that of the Austrian empire within the period during which it may be hoped that Mr. Hülsemann may yet remain in the honorable

[1] From *The Writings and Speeches of Daniel Webster* (Boston, 1903), XII, pp. 165–178.

discharge of his duties to his government. Its navigation and commerce are hardly exceeded by the oldest and most commercial nations, its maritime means and its maritime power may be seen by Austria itself, in all seas where she has ports, as well as they may be seen, also, in all other quarters of the globe. Life, liberty, property, and all personal rights, are amply secured to all citizens, and protected by just and stable laws; and credit, public and private, is as well established as in any government of Continental Europe; and the country, in all its interests and concerns, partakes most largely in all the improvements and progress which distinguish the age. Certainly, the United States may be pardoned, even by those who profess adherence to the principles of absolute government, if they entertain an ardent affection for those popular forms of political organization which have so rapidly advanced their own prosperity and happiness, and enabled them, in so short a period, to bring their country, and the hemisphere to which it belongs, to the notice and respectful regard, not to say the admiration, of the civilized world. Nevertheless, the United States have abstained, at all times, from acts of interference with the political changes of Europe. They cannot, however, fail to cherish always a lively interest in the fortunes of nations struggling for institutions like their own. But this sympathy, so far from being necessarily a hostile feeling toward any of the parties to these great national struggles, is quite consistent with amicable relations with them all. The Hungarian people are three or four times as numerous as the inhabitants of these United States were when the American Revolution broke out. They possess, in a distinct language, and in other respects, important elements of a separate nationality, which the Anglo-Saxon race in this country did not possess; and if the United States wish success to countries contending for popular constitutions and national independence, it is only because they regard such constitutions and such national independence, not as imaginary, but as real blessings. They claim no right, however, to take part in the struggles of foreign powers in order to promote these ends. . . .

— 15 —

PERRY'S TREATY WITH JAPAN, MARCH 31, 1854[1]

When Commodore Perry sailed into the Bay of Yedo in the summer of 1853, Japan was tightly sealed against Western influences save for a single port to which only Chinese and Dutch traders had access. He announced his purpose of negotiating a treaty and upon his return the following February found the Shogun's government prepared to enter into diplomatic discussions. Perry's success has been attributed to the impressiveness of his task force, which first numbered four well-armed ships, then nine, and included two steam sloops-of-war; and to Perry's own calculated haughtiness and inaccessibility. However, the Japanese government had knowledge that Western powers had used force on China and might soon train their guns on Japan. The concessions granted in this first treaty were not impressive, but Perry opened the door enough to admit the agents of the United States and other powers, and more far-reaching terms were obtained in 1857 and 1858.

✓   ✓   ✓

The United States of America and the Empire of Japan, desiring to establish firm, lasting, and sincere friendship between the two nations, have resolved to fix, in a manner clear and positive, by means of a treaty or general convention of peace and amity, the rules which shall in future be mutually observed in the intercourse of their respective countries; for which most desirable object the President of the United States has conferred full powers on his Commissioner, Matthew Calbraith Perry, Special Ambassador of the United States to Japan, and the August Sovereign of Japan has given similar full

[1] From Malloy, *Treaties, Conventions, etc.,* I, pp. 996-998.

powers to his Commissioners, Hayashi, Daigaku-no-kami; Ido, Prince of Tsus-Sima; Izawa, Prince of Mima-saki; and Udono, Member of the Board of Revenue. And the said Commissioners, after having exchanged their said full powers, and duly considered the premises, have agreed to the following articles:

ARTICLE I. There shall be a perfect, permanent, and universal peace, and a sincere and cordial amity between the United States of America on the one part, and the Empire of Japan on the other part, and between their people respectively, without exception of persons or places.

ARTICLE II. The port of Simoda, in the principality of Idzu, and the port of Hakodade, in the principality of Matsmai, are granted by the Japanese as ports for the reception of American ships, where they can be supplied with wood, water, provisions, and coal, and other articles their necessities may require, as far as the Japanese have them. . . .

ARTICLE III. Whenever ships of the United States are thrown or wrecked on the coast of Japan, the Japanese vessels will assist them, and carry their crews to Simoda, or Hakodade, and hand them over to their countrymen, appointed to receive them; whatever articles the ship-wrecked men may have preserved shall likewise be restored, and the expenses incurred in the rescue and support of Americans and Japanese who may thus be thrown upon the shores of either nation are not to be refunded.

ARTICLE IV. Those shipwrecked persons and other citizens of the United States shall be free as in other countries, and not subjected to confinement, but shall be amenable to just laws.

ARTICLE V. Shipwrecked men and other citizens of the United States, temporarily living at Simoda and Hakodade, shall not be subject to such restrictions and confinement as the Dutch and Chinese are at Nagasaki, but shall be free at Simoda to go where they please within the limits of seven Japanese miles (or ri) from a small island in the harbor of Simoda marked on the accompanying chart hereto appended; and shall in like manner be free to go where they please at Hakodade, within limits to be defined after the visit of the United States squadron to that place.

ARTICLE VI. If there be any other sort of goods wanted, or any business which shall require to be arranged, there shall be careful deliberation between the parties in order to settle such matters.

ARTICLE VII. It is agreed that ships of the United States resorting to the ports open to them shall be permitted to exchange gold and silver coin and articles of goods for other articles of goods, under such regulations as shall be temporarily established. . . .

ARTICLE VIII. Wood, water, provisions, coal and goods required, shall only be procured through the agency of Japanese officers appointed for that purpose, and in no other manner.

ARTICLE IX. It is agreed that if at any future day the Government of Japan shall grant to any other nation or nations privileges and advantages which are not herein granted to the United States and the citizens thereof, that these same privileges and advantages shall be granted likewise to the United States and to the citizens thereof, without any consultation or delay.

ARTICLE X. Ships of the United States shall be permitted to resort to no other ports in Japan but Simoda and Hakodade, unless in distress or forced by stress of weather.

ARTICLE XI. There shall be appointed, by the Government of the United States, Consuls or Agents to reside in Simoda, at any time after the expiration of eighteen months from the date of the signing of this treaty; provided that either of the two Governments deem such arrangement necessary. . . .

CUBA COVETED,
DECEMBER 6, 1858[1]

As American minister to Great Britain, James Buchanan had signed the Ostend Manifesto of October 15, 1854, which urged the acquisition of Cuba by the United States either by purchase or, as a last resort, by war. The partisan outcry over this advice, when it became known, dimmed the hopes of southern annexationists; but the Democratic party continued to covet Cuba, and four years later Buchanan, as President, stressed its value to the United States and asked Congress for funds for its purchase. Neither Congress nor the nation was then interested in distant or offshore islands. This statement appears in President Buchanan's second annual message to Congress.

✓   ✓   ✓

Fellow-Citizens of the Senate and House of Representatives:

. . . With Spain our relations remain in an unsatisfactory condition. . . .

Spanish officials under the direct control of the Captain-General of Cuba have insulted our national flag and in repeated instances have from time to time inflicted injuries on the persons and property of our citizens. These have given birth to numerous claims against the Spanish Government . . . (but) all our attempts to obtain redress have been baffled and defeated. . . .

One alleged cause for procrastination in the examination and adjustment of our claims arises from an obstacle which it is the duty of the Spanish Government to remove. Whilst the Captain-General of Cuba is invested

[1] From Richardson, ed., *Messages and Papers of the Presidents,* V, pp. 508-511.

with general despotic authority in the government of that island, the power is withheld from him to examine and redress wrongs committed by officials under his control on citizens of the United States. . . . Cuba is almost within sight of our shores. . . . It is therefore a great grievance that when any difficulty occurs, no matter how unimportant, which might be readily settled at the moment, we should be obliged to resort to Madrid, especially when the very first step to be taken there is to refer it back to Cuba.

The truth is that Cuba, in its existing colonial condition, is a constant source of injury and annoyance to the American people. It is the only spot in the civilized world where the African slave trade is tolerated, and . . . as long as this market shall remain open there can be no hope for the civilization of benighted Africa. . . .

It has been made known to the world by my predecessors that the United States have on several occasions endeavored to acquire Cuba from Spain by honorable negotiation. If this were accomplished, the last relic of the African slave trade would instantly disappear. We would not, if we could, acquire Cuba in any other manner. This is due to our national character. All the territory which we have acquired since the origin of the Government has been by fair purchase from France, Spain, and Mexico or by the free and voluntary act of the independent State of Texas in blending her destinies with our own. This course we shall ever pursue, unless circumstances should occur which we do not now anticipate, rendering a departure from it clearly justifiable under the imperative and overruling law of self-preservation. . . .

The publicity which has been given to our former negotiations upon this subject and the large appropriation which may be required to effect the purpose render it expedient before making another attempt to renew the negotiation that I should lay the whole subject before Congress. This is especially necessary, as it may become indispensable to success that I should be intrusted with the means of making an advance to the Spanish Government immediately after the signing of the treaty, without awaiting the ratification of it by the Senate. I am encouraged to make this suggestion by the example of Mr.

Jefferson previous to the purchase of Louisiana from France and by that of Mr. Polk in view of the acquisition of territory from Mexico. I refer the whole subject to Congress and commend it to their careful consideration. . . .

— 17 —

MONROE DOCTRINE
IN PRACTICE:
MEXICO, 1865-1866[1]

In the early months of the American Civil War, Great Britain, France and Spain intervened in Mexico to protect property rights and lives of their nationals. From this beginning, Napoleon III turned Mexico into a French protectorate and set up the Austrian Archduke Maximilian to rule as emperor. The enterprise was viewed with indignation in the United States, but Secretary of State William H. Seward waited until the Civil War was over before he risked a challenge to France. On November 6, 1865, he sent the American minister in Paris the despatch printed below for Napoleon's government. Other factors influenced Napoleon's decision to withdraw his troops from Mexico, and leave Maximilian to his tragic fate; but the position taken by the United States, and firmly maintained in later despatches, made his retreat all but inevitable. The Monroe doctrine is not mentioned in Seward's notes to France, but the outcome of its application enhanced its authority and prestige at home and abroad.

✦   ✦   ✦

[1] From *Papers Relating to Foreign Affairs, 1865-66* (Washington 1866), Part III, pp. 421-422.

November 6, 1865

Mr. Seward to Mr. Bigelow

. . . The presence and operations of a French army in Mexico, and its maintenance of an authority there, resting on force and not the free will of the people of Mexico, is a cause of serious concern to the United States. Nevertheless, the objection of the United States is still broader, and includes the authority itself which the French army is thus maintaining. The authority itself is in direct antagonism to the policy of this government and the principles upon which it is founded.

Every day's experience of the operations only adds some new confirmation of the justice of the views which this government expressed at the time the attempt to institute that authority first became known. The United States have hitherto practiced the utmost frankness on that subject.

They still regard the effort to establish permanently a foreign and imperial government in Mexico as disallowable and impracticable. For these reasons they could not now agree to compromise the position they have hitherto assumed. They are not prepared to recognize, or to pledge themselves hereafter to recognize, any political institutions in Mexico which are in opposition to the republican government with which we have so long and so constantly maintained relations of amity and friendship. . . .

— 18 —

CIVIL WAR BLOCKADE: CASE OF THE *BERMUDA* DECEMBER, 1865[1]

In an unaccustomed role during the American Civil War, the United States government demanded that Euro-

[1] From J. W. Wallace, *Cases Argued and Adjudged in the Supreme Court of the United States* (New York, 1909), III, pp. 542-558.

pean powers observe the obligations of neutrality and claimed its full rights as a belligerent. Thus the United States demanded that Britain pay heavily for the damage done by Confederate cruisers built in English shipyards (see Alabama Claims, May 8, 1871), *and had no hesitation in applying the British doctrine of "continuous voyage" in its blockade of southern ports. American naval vessels stopped British merchant-men and took them in if their cargo or papers convicted them of unneutral intent, even if their immediate destination was a British port in Bermuda or Nassau. The* Bermuda, *flying the Union Jack but actually owned by a Charleston firm, was captured on April 27, 1862, four days out of Bermuda en route to another British island or blockaded southern port. The United States Supreme Court later upheld the decision to confiscate both ship and cargo largely on the "continuous voyage" concept. Although British interests had been deeply involved in supplying the Confederacy with arms, the British government could not protest a ruling that enhanced the utility of seapower in time of war.*

✓   ✓   ✓

The Chief Justice [*Salmon P. Chase*] delivered the opinion of the Court. . . .

The questions arising upon the ownership of the steamship, will first be disposed of.

She was built in 1861, on the eastern coast of England, at Stockton-upon-Tees. On the 1st of August in that year, Edwin Haigh (a British subject) made the declaration of ownership required by the British Merchants' Shipping Act of 1854. . . .

All these transactions, prior to capture, and at the time of capture, repel the conclusion that Haigh was the owner. . . . All the papers and all the circumstances indicate rather that a sale was made in Charleston under the power, by which the beneficial control and real ownership were transferred to John Fraser and Co. (of Charleston), while the apparent title, by the British papers, was suffered to remain in Haigh as a cover. . . .

We are obliged to think that the ownership of Haigh was a pretence, and that the vessel was rightly condemned as enemy property.

We will next consider the questions relating both to vessel and cargo . . .

How, then, was the *Bermuda* employed? In what trade, and under what control and direction?

The theory of the counsel for Haigh is that she was a neutral ship, carrying a neutral cargo, in good faith, from one neutral port to another neutral port; and they insist that the description of cargo, if neutral, and in a neutral ship, and on a neutral voyage, cannot be inquired into in the courts of a belligerent.

We agree to this. Neutral trade is entitled to protection in all courts. . . .

But if it is intended to affirm that a neutral ship may take on a contraband cargo ostensibly for a neutral port, but destined in reality for a belligerent port, either by the same ship or by another, without becoming liable, from the commencement to the end of the voyage, to seizure, in order to the confiscation of the cargo, we do not agree to it. . . .

It is not denied that a large part of her cargo was contraband in the narrowest sense of that word. One portion was made up of Blakely cannon and other guns in cases, of howitzers, of cannon not in cases, of carriages for guns, of shells, fuses, and other like articles—near eighty tons in all; and of seven cases of pistols, twenty-one cases of swords, seventy barrels of cartridges, 300 whole barrels, 78 half-barrels and 283 quarter-barrels of gunpowder. . . .

The character of this cargo makes its ulterior, if not direct, destination to a rebel port quite certain. . . .

The interposition of a neutral port between neutral departure and belligerent destination has always been a favorite resort of contraband carriers and blockade-runners. But it never avails them when the ultimate destination is ascertained. A transportation from one point to another remains continuous, so long as intent remains unchanged, no matter what stoppages or transshipments intervene. . . .

There remains the question whether the *Bermuda,* on the supposition that she was really a neutral ship, should be condemned for the conveyance of contraband. For, in general, as we have seen, a neutral may convey contraband to a belligerent, subject to no liability except seizure in order to confiscation of the offending goods. The ship is not forfeited, nor are non-offending parts of the cargo. . . .

The rule, however, requires good faith on the part of the neutral, and does not protect a ship where good faith is wanting. . . .

We cannot doubt that the *Bermuda* was justly liable to condemnation for the conveyance of contraband goods destined to a belligerent port, under circumstances of fraud and bad faith, which make the owner, if Haigh was the owner, responsible for unneutral participation in the war. . . .

The cargo, having all been consigned to enemies, and most of it contraband, must share the fate of the ship. . . .

— 19 —

THE *ALABAMA* CLAIMS: TREATY OF WASHINGTON, MAY 8, 1871 [1]

When the Civil War began, Great Britain conferred belligerent rights on the Confederacy by proclaiming its own neutrality, and the Confederate government soon began placing orders for warships with English shipbuilders. Since supplying warships to either belligerent would have been a violation of British neutrality, the ships were built in English yards and fitted out for war at distant and obscure ports. Well-documented protests of the American minister, Charles Francis Adams, finally impelled the Palmerston government to stop building a

[1] From Malloy, *Treaties, Conventions, etc.,* I, pp. 700-716.

Confederate navy; but the Alabama *and other commerce-raiders were already deep in their destructive careers. At the end of the war Great Britain rejected an American proposal that claims for damages be submitted to arbitration, and anti-British sentiment in the Senate led to the proposal that Britain meet direct and indirect claims by the cession of Canada. Calmer judgment finally prevailed on both sides of the Atlantic, and arbitration was agreed to in the Treaty of Washington. The arbitrators threw out the fantastic indirect claims and awarded damages of $15,000,000. This outcome was helpful to Anglo-American relations, served to define the duties of neutrality, and advanced the cause of international arbitration.*

✦   ✦   ✦

ARTICLE I. Whereas differences have arisen between the Government of the United States and the Government of Her Britannic Majesty, and still exist, growing out of the acts committed by the several vessels which have given rise to the claims generically known as the "*Alabama* Claims":

And whereas Her Britannic Majesty has authorized her High Commissioners and Plenipotentiaries to express, in a friendly spirit, the regret felt by Her Majesty's Government for the escape, under whatever circumstances, of the *Alabama* and other vessels from British ports, and for the depredations committed by those vessels:

Now, in order to remove and adjust all complaints and claims on the part of the United States, and to provide for the speedy settlement of such claims which are not admitted by Her Britannic Majesty's Government, the high contracting parties agree that all the said claims, growing out of acts committed by the aforesaid vessels, and generically known as the "*Alabama* Claims," shall be referred to a tribunal of arbitration to be composed of five Arbitrators, to be appointed in the following manner: One shall be named by the President of the United States; one shall be named by Her Britannic Majesty; His Majesty the King of Italy shall be requested to name one; the President of the Swiss Confederation shall be requested to name one; and His Majesty the Emperor of Brazil shall be requested to name one. . . .

ARTICLE II. The Arbitrators shall meet at Geneva, in

Switzerland, at the earliest convenient day after they shall have been named, and shall proceed impartially and carefully to examine and decide all questions that shall be laid before them on the part of the Governments of the United States and Her Britannic Majesty respectively. All questions considered by the tribunal, including the final award, shall be decided by a majority of all the Arbitrators. . . .

ARTICLE VI. In deciding the matters submitted to the Arbitrators, they shall be governed by the following three rules, which are agreed upon by the high contracting parties as rules to be taken as applicable to the case, and by such principles of international law not inconsistent therewith as the Arbitrators shall determine to have been applicable to the case.

Rules

A neutral Government is bound—First, to use due diligence to prevent the fitting out, arming, or equipping, within its jurisdiction, of any vessel which it has reasonable ground to believe is intended to cruise or to carry on war against a Power with which it is at peace; and also to use like diligence to prevent the departure from its jurisdiction of any vessel intended to cruise or carry on war as above, such vessel having been specially adapted, in whole or in part, within such jurisdiction, to warlike use. Secondly, not to permit or suffer either belligerent to make use of its ports or waters as a base of naval operations against the other, or for the purpose of the renewal or augmentation of military supplies or arms, or the recruitment of men. Thirdly, to exercise due diligence in its own ports and waters, and, as to all persons within its jurisdiction, to prevent any violation of the foregoing obligations and duties. . . .

ARTICLE VII. . . . The said tribunal shall first determine as to each vessel separately whether Great Britain has, by any act or omission, failed to fulfill any of the duties set forth in the foregoing three rules, or recognized by the principles of international law not inconsistent with such rules, and shall certify such fact as to each of the said vessels. In case the tribunal find that Great Britain has failed to fulfil any duty or duties as aforesaid, it may, if it think proper, proceed to award a sum in gross to be paid by Great Britain to the United States for all the claims referred to it. . . .

ARTICLE X. In case the tribunal finds that Great Britain has failed to fulfil any duty or duties as aforesaid, and does not award a sum in gross, the high contracting parties agree that a board of assessors shall be appointed to ascertain and determine what claims are valid, and what amount or amounts shall be paid by Great Britain to the United States. . . .

ARTICLE XI. The high contracting parties engage to consider the result of the proceedings of the tribunal of arbitration and of the board of Assessors, should such board be appointed, as a full, perfect, and final settlement of all the claims hereinbefore referred to. . . .

— 20 —

CHINESE EXCLUSION ACT MAY 6, 1882 [1]

The importation of Chinese laborers facilitated railway-building in the Far West in the 1860's, but later led to anti-Chinese riots in California and demands that coolie labor be excluded. A Chinese-American treaty of 1868 guaranteed most-favored-nation treatment for Chinese nationals, excepting the right of naturalization; but China agreed in an immigration treaty of 1880 that the United States might "regulate, limit, or suspend" Chinese immigration, though "not absolutely prohibit it." The suspension of the admission of Chinese labor by Congress was renewed periodically, but in 1943, at the time the United States tore up its unequal treaties with China, Congress

[1] From *Statutes at Large of the United States* (Washington, 1883), XXII, pp. 58-61.

*removed the ban on Chinese immigrants and placed them
on a regular quota basis, as well as granting the right of
naturalization.*

✓   ✓   ✓

Whereas, in the opinion of the Government of the
United States the coming of Chinese laborers to this
country endangers the good order of certain localities
within the territory thereof; Therefore,

Be it enacted by the Senate and House of Representatives of the United States in Congress assembled, That
from and after the expiration of ninety days next after the
passage of this act, and until the expiration of ten years
next after the passage of this act, the coming of Chinese
laborers to the United States be, and the same is hereby,
suspended; and during such suspension it shall not be
lawful for any Chinese laborer to come, or having so
come after the expiration of said ninety days, to remain
in the United States. . . .

Section 14. That hereafter no State court or court of
the United States shall admit Chinese to citizenship; and
all laws in conflict with this act are hereby repealed. . . .

— 21 —

INTER-AMERICAN CONFERENCE, 1889-1890[1]

*The Pan American movement owes much to James G.
Blaine, Secretary of State under three Republican presidents. His effort to convene an Inter-American conference
in 1881 came to nothing when he was relieved of office
and his successor withdrew the invitations that had been*

[1] From *Foreign Relations of the United States, 1888*, Pt. II,
pp. 1658-1659.

sent out. Blaine continued to plead the cause of Pan Americanism, and in 1888 Congress requested President Cleveland to call a conference. Invitations were sent out by Thomas F. Bayard, Secretary of State, and by the time the delegates arrived Cleveland had been succeeded by Benjamin Harrison. Blaine was again at the State Department and presided over the conference of eighteen American states. Cordiality was high, and the delegates were given a six-weeks' tour of the country, but the results of the meeting fell far short of expectations. However, the conference established a Union of American Republics,[1] later named the Pan American Union; and an important precedent had been established for the discussion of questions of common interest to all American nations.

✓   ✓   ✓

July 13, 1888

(*To the diplomatic representatives accredited to the independent American states.*)

Sir: At the present session of Congress an act was passed, to which the President's approval was given on the 24th of May last, by the terms of which the President is requested and authorized—

To invite the several governments of the Republics of Mexico, Central and South America, Hayti, San Domingo, and the Empire of Brazil, to join the United States in a conference to be held in Washington, in the United States, at such time as he may deem proper, in the year 1889. . . .

It also provided in the act referred to that in forwarding the invitation to the said Governments, the President of the United States shall set forth that the conference is called to consider—

First. Measures that shall tend to preserve and promote the prosperity of the several American states.

Second. Measures toward the formation of an American customs union, under which the trade of the American nations with each other shall, so far as possible and profitable, be promoted.

---

[1] During the conference the Empire of Brazil had quietly become a republic.

Third. The establishment of regular and frequent communication between the ports of the several American States . . .

Fourth. The establishment of a uniform system of customs regulations in each of the independent American States. . . .

Fifth. The adoption of a uniform system of weights and measures, and laws to protect the patent-rights, copyrights, and trademarks of citizens of either country in the other, and for the extradition of criminals.

Sixth. The adoption of a common silver coin, to be issued by each Government, the same to be legal tender in all commercial transactions between the citizens of all of the American States.

Seventh. An agreement upon and recommendation for adoption to their respective Governments of a definite plan of arbitration of all questions, disputes, and differences that may now or hereafter exist between them, to the end that all difficulties and disputes between such nations may be peaceably settled and wars prevented.

Eighth. And to consider such other subjects relating to the welfare of the several states represented as may be presented by any of said states which are hereby invited to participate in said conference.

I have to call your particular attention to the scope and object of the conference suggested, which, as will be observed, is consultative and recommendatory only. . . .

By direction, therefore, of the President of the United States and in his name, you will tender to the Government of—a cordial invitation to be represented by such number of delegates as may seem convenient at the international conference to be convened as aforesaid in the city of Washington, on Wednesday, the 2d of October of the coming year, 1889. . . .

T. F. BAYARD

McKINLEY'S WAR MESSAGE
APRIL 11, 1898 [1]

From desiring almost any peaceful solution of the Cuban problem, President McKinley was brought by direct and atmospheric pressures to the choice of war. He arrived at this decision just as the Spanish government yielded to the American demand for an armistice in Cuba as a preliminary to peace talks. McKinley mentioned the Spanish concession at the end of his provocative war message, but he did not add that the American minister in Madrid was convinced that the Cuban question could be solved to our satisfaction by diplomatic means. Whether the minister was right may be questioned, but the progress the United States had already made through diplomacy, particularly the recent Spanish agreement to suspend hostilities in Cuba, suggested that McKinley had at least one alternative to war. Congress, however, was in a mood for action.

✓   ✓   ✓

To the Congress of the United States:

Obedient to that precept of the Constitution which commands the President to give from time to time to the Congress information of the state of the Union and to recommend to their consideration such measures as he shall judge necessary and expedient, it becomes my duty to now address your body with regard to the grave crisis that has arisen in the relations of the United States to Spain by reason of the warfare that for more than three years has raged in the neighboring island of Cuba. . . .

The war in Cuba is of such nature that, short of subjugation or extermination, a final military victory for

[1] From Richardson, ed., *Messages and Papers of the Presidents*, X, pp. 56-67.

either side seems impracticable. The alternative lies in the physical exhaustion of the one or the other party, or perhaps of both—a condition which in effect ended the ten years' war by the truce of Zanjon. The prospect of such a protraction and conclusion of the present strife is a contingency hardly to be contemplated with equanimity by the civilized world, and least of all by the United States, affected and injured as we are, deeply and intimately, by its very existence.

Realizing this, it appeared to be my duty, in a spirit of true friendliness, no less to Spain than to the Cubans, who have so much to lose by the prolongation of the struggle, to seek to bring about an immediate termination of the war. To this end I submitted on the 27th ultimo, as a result of much representation and correspondence, through the United States minister at Madrid, propositions to the Spanish Government looking to an armistice until October 1 for the negotiation of peace with the good offices of the President. . . .

The reply of the Spanish cabinet was received on the night of the 31st ultimo. It offered, as the means to bring about peace in Cuba, to confide the preparation thereof to the insular parliament, inasmuch as the concurrence of that body would be necessary to reach a final result, it being, however, understood that the powers reserved by the constitution to the central Government are not lessened or diminished. As the Cuban parliament does not meet until the 4th of May next, the Spanish Government would not object for its part to accept at once a suspension of hostilities if asked for by the insurgents from the general in chief, to whom it would pertain in such case to determine the duration and conditions of the armistice. . . .

With this last overture in the direction of immediate peace, and its disappointing reception by Spain, the Executive is brought to the end of his effort.

In my annual message of December last I said:

> Of the untried measures there remain only: Recognition of the insurgents as belligerents; recognition of the independence of Cuba; neutral intervention to end the war by imposing a rational compromise between the contestants, and intervention in favor of one or the other party. I speak not of forcible annex-

ation, for that can not be thought of. That, by our code of morality, would be criminal aggression.

Thereupon I reviewed these alternatives in the light of President Grant's measured words, uttered in 1875, when, after seven years of sanguinary, destructive, and cruel hostilities in Cuba, he reached the conclusion that the recognition of the independence of Cuba was impracticable and indefensible and that the recognition of belligerence was not warranted by the facts according to the tests of public law. . . .

There remain the alternative forms of intervention to end the war, either as an impartial neutral, by imposing a rational compromise between the contestants, or as the active ally of the one party or the other. . . .

The grounds for such intervention may be briefly summarized as follows:

First. In the cause of humanity and to put an end to the barbarities, bloodshed, starvation, and horrible miseries now existing there, and which the parties to the conflict are either unable or unwilling to stop or mitigate. It is no answer to say this is all in another country belonging to another nation, and is therefore none of our business. It is specially our duty, for it is right at our door.

Second. We owe it to our citizens in Cuba to afford them that protection and indemnity for life and property which no government there can or will afford, and to that end to terminate the conditions that deprive them of legal protection.

Third. The right to intervene may be justified by the very serious injury to the commerce, trade, and business of our people and by the wanton destruction of property and devastation of the island.

Fourth, and which is of the utmost importance. The present condition of affairs in Cuba is a constant menace to our peace and entails upon the Government an enormous expense. . . .

These elements of danger and disorder already pointed out have been strikingly illustrated by a tragic event which has deeply and justly moved the American people. I have already transmitted to Congress the report of the naval court of inquiry on the destruction of the battle ship *Maine* in the harbor of Havana during the night of the 15th of February. The destruction of that noble vessel has filled the national heart with inexpressible horror. Two hundred and fifty-eight brave sailors and marines and two officers of our Navy, reposing in the fancied security of a friendly harbor, have been hurled to death, grief and want brought to their homes and sorrow to the nation. . . . The destruction of the *Maine*, by whatever exterior cause, is a patent and impressive proof of a state of things in Cuba that is intolerable. That condition is thus shown to be such that the Spanish Government can not assure safety and security to a vessel of the American Navy in the harbor of Havana on a mission of peace, and rightfully there. . . .

The long trial has proved that the object for which Spain has waged the war can not be attained. The fire of insurrection may flame or may smolder with varying seasons, but it has not been and it is plain that it can not be extinguished by present methods. The only hope of relief and repose from a condition which can no longer be endured is the enforced pacification of Cuba. In the name of humanity, in the name of civilization, in behalf of endangered American interests, which give us the right and the duty to speak and to act, the war in Cuba must stop.

In view of these facts and of these considerations I ask the Congress to authorize and empower the President to take measures to secure a full and final termination of hostilities between the Government of Spain and the people of Cuba, and to secure in the island the establishment of a stable government, capable of maintaining order and observing its international obligations, insuring peace and tranquillity and the security of its citizens as well as our own, and to use the military and naval forces of the United States as may be necessary for these purposes . . .

The issue is now with the Congress. It is a solemn responsibility. I have exhausted every effort to relieve the intolerable condition of affairs which is at our doors. Prepared to execute every obligation imposed upon me by the Constitution and the law, I await your action.

Yesterday, and since the preparation of the foregoing message, official information was received by me that the latest decree of the Queen Regent of Spain directs General Blanco, in order to prepare and facilitate peace, to proclaim a suspension of hostilities, the duration and details of which have not yet been communicated to me.

This fact, with every other pertinent consideration, will, I am sure, have your just and careful attention in the solemn deliberations upon which you are about to enter. If this measure attains a successful result, then our aspirations as a Christian, peace-loving people will be realized. If it fails, it will be only another justification for our contemplated action.

WILLIAM McKINLEY

— 23 —

CUBAN RESOLUTIONS WITH THE TELLER AMENDMENT, APRIL 20, 1898[1]

Instead of declaring war on Spain, Congress responded to McKinley's message by adopting four resolutions which made war inevitable unless Spain at once recognized Cuba's independence and withdrew. The fourth resolution, introduced by Senator Teller of Colorado, and known as the Teller Amendment, was favored by the sugar-beet interests, but gave the American effort an air of disinterestedness which the annexation of other Spanish islands did not bear out. The vote on the Resolutions was fairly close in the Senate, 42 to 35, and swept the House, 311 to 6. Spain declared war upon receiving news of the resolutions and Congress then formally declared war.

✓　　　　　✓　　　　　✓

[1] From *Statutes at Large of the United States of America*, XXX, pp. 738-739.

Whereas the abhorrent conditions which have existed for more than three years in the Island of Cuba, so near our own borders, have shocked the moral sense of the people of the United States, have been a disgrace to Christian civilization, culminating, as they have, in the destruction of a United States battle ship, with two hundred and sixty-six of its officers and crew, while on a friendly visit in the harbor of Havana, and can not longer be endured, as has been set forth by the President of the United States in his message to Congress of April 11, 1898, upon which the action of Congress was invited: Therefore, *Resolved by the Senate and House of Representatives of the United States of America in Congress assembled,*

First. That the people of the Island of Cuba are, and of right ought to be, free and independent.

Second. That it is the duty of the United States to demand, and the Government of the United States does hereby demand, that the Government of Spain at once relinquish its authority and government in the Island of Cuba and withdraw its land and naval forces from Cuba and Cuban waters.

Third. That the President of the United States be, and he hereby is, directed and empowered to use the entire land and naval forces of the United States, and to call into the actual service of the United States the militia of the several states, to such extent as may be necessary to carry these resolutions into effect.

Fourth. That the United States hereby disclaims any disposition or intention to exercise sovereignty, jurisdiction, or control over said Island except for the pacification thereof, and asserts its determination, when that is accomplished, to leave the government and control of the Island to its people.

THE ECONOMICS OF
EXPANSION, 1898 [1]

*In his annual message of December, 1897, McKinley
had said flatly that the forcible annexation of Cuba
would be "criminal aggression," but in the following
year he yielded to the claims of Manifest Destiny in
annexing Puerto Rico, Guam, and the Philippines. The
energetic "expansionists of 1898" would probably not
have made a convert of McKinley had they not already
made a strong impress on the American mind. The great
debate between the imperialists and the anti-imperialists
was marked by ability and intensity, and it is to be noted
that the distinguished Americans who opposed expansion
scored a posthumous victory in the Philippines' eventual
independence. But at the time the concepts of national
duty, inevitability, and Manifest Destiny, which were the
empire-builders' weapons, were all but impervious to
reason. Charles Arthur Conant here employs notions of
"irresistible tendency," necessity and inevitability to bolster a fascinating economic case for expansion. Conant
was Washington correspondent of the* New York Journal
of Commerce *with the specialty of finance. This article,
entitled "The Economic Basis of Imperialism," appeared
in the* North American Review *of September, 1898.*

✓ ✓ ✓

The instinctive tendency of a race or civilization often
outruns the wisdom of its leaders. Whether for good or
ill, the inborn tendencies of race . . . prevail by a sort
of instinct. Other races in seeking to pursue the same
paths by imitation have stumbled and gone astray. But

[1] From the *North American Review*, CLXVII (Sept., 1898),
pp. 326-340.

when the current of race or national tendencies runs strongly in a given channel it is apt to override alike the misgivings of its sympathizers and the protests and resistance of those who would obstruct it. The United States today seem about to enter upon a path marked out for them as the children of the Anglo-Saxon race, not yet traversed because there has been so much to do at home. Almost as if by magic, the importance of naval power as the advance agent of commercial supremacy has flashed upon the mind of the country. The irresistible tendency to expansion, which leads the growing tree to burst every barrier, which drove the Goths, the Vandals, and finally our Saxon ancestors in successive and irresistible waves over the decadent provinces of Rome, seems again in operation, demanding new outlets for American capital and new opportunities for American enterprise.

This new movement is not a matter of sentiment. It is the result of a natural law of economic and race development. The great civilized peoples have today at their command the means of developing the decadent nations of the world. This means, in its material aspects, is the great excess of saved capital which is the result of machine production. It is proposed to point out in this article how great this excess is at the present time, how profoundly it is disturbing economic conditions in the older countries, and how necessary to the salvation of these countries is an outlet for their surplus savings, if the entire fabric of the present economic order is not to be shaken by a social revolution. The law of self preservation, as well as that of the survival of the fittest, is urging our people on in a path which is undoubtedly a departure from the policy of the past, but which is inevitably marked out by the new conditions and requirements of the present. . . .

The conditions of the early part of the century have changed. Capital is no longer needed in excess of the supply, but it is becoming congested. The benefits of saving have been inculcated with such effect for many decades that savings accumulate beyond the development of new demands for capital which are legitimate, and are becoming a menace to the economic future of the great industrial countries. . . .

There are three important solutions of this enormous congestion of capital in excess of legitimate demand. One of these is the socialistic solution of the abandonment of saving, the application of the whole earnings of the laborer to current consumption, and the support of old age out of taxes levied upon the production of the community. It will be long before this solution will be accepted in a comprehensive form in any modern civilized state. The second solution is the creation of new demands at home for the absorption of capital. This has occurred at several previous stages of the world's history and is likely to continue as long as human desires continue expansible. But there has never been a time before when the proportion of capital to be absorbed was so great in proportion to possible new demands. Means for building more bicycle factories than are needed, and for laying more electric railways than are able to pay dividends, have been taken out of current savings within the last few years, without producing any marked effect upon their amount and without doing more, at the most, than to stay the downward course of the rate of interest. Aside from the waste of capital in war, which is only a form of consumption, there remains, therefore, as the final resource, the equipment of new countries with the means of production and exchange. . . .

Such countries have yet to be equipped with the mechanism of production and of luxury, which has been created in the progressive countries by the savings of recent generations. They have not only to obtain buildings and machinery—the necessary elements in producing machine-made goods—but they have to build their roads, drain their marshes, dam their rivers, build aqueducts for their water supplies and sewers for their towns and cities. Asia and Africa are the most promising of these countries. . . .

The United States cannot afford to adhere to a policy of isolation while other nations are reaching out for the command of these new markets. The United States are still large users of foreign capital, but American investors are not willing to see the return upon their investments reduced to the European level. Interest rates have greatly declined here within the last five years. New markets and new opportunities for investment must be found if surplus capital is to be profitably employed.

... The writer is not an advocate of "imperialism" from sentiment, but does not fear the name if it means only that the United States shall assert their right to free markets in all the old countries which are being opened to the surplus resources of the capitalistic countries and thereby given the benefits of modern civilization. Whether this policy carries with it the direct government of groups of half-savage islands may be a subject for argument, but upon the economic side of the question there is but one choice—either to enter by some means upon the competition for the employment of American capital and enterprise in these countries, or to continue the needless duplication of existing means of production and communication, with the glut of unconsumed products, the convulsions followed by trade stagnation, and the steadily declining return upon investments which this policy will invoke. . . .

— 25 —

OPEN DOOR IN CHINA, 1899-1900

The sequel to China's ignominious defeat by Japan in 1894-1895 was a scramble among the western powers for economic concessions, spheres of influence and leaseholds in the amorphous Chinese Empire. This development threatened the Open Door policy by which both Great Britain and the United States had sought to safeguard the rights of their own traders. Britain deplored the new raiding, but in 1898 staked out her own claims. In 1899 McKinley's Secretary of State, John Hay, invited Great Britain, Germany, France, Italy, Russia and

Japan, the powers that had moved in on China, to declare that they would keep the door open in their respective Chinese spheres (Document A). *The replies expressed varying degrees of self-denial, but Hay felt that he was now justified in proclaiming the Open Door policy in effect for all the interested powers* (Document B). *A few months later, at the peak of anti-foreign violence in China, known as the Boxer Rebellion, Hay sent around a statement of United States policy which went beyond the Open Door to the preservation of China's "territorial and administrative entity"* (Document C). *This second circular note also evoked relatively agreeable replies; but the two diplomatic maneuvers, though they gave Hay exaggerated prestige at the time, had slight influence on the course of events in China.*

✓   ✓   ✓

A. HAY'S OPEN DOOR PROPOSALS

Mr. Choate, United States ambassador to Great Britain, to Lord Salisbury, Prime Minister and Secretary of State for Foreign Affairs, September 22, 1899[1]

. . . It is the sincere desire of my Government that the interests of its citizens may not be prejudiced through exclusive treatment by any of the controlling powers within their respective "spheres of interests" in China, and it hopes to retain there an open market for all the world's commerce, remove dangerous sources of international irritation, and thereby hasten united action of the Powers at Pekin to promote administrative reforms so greatly needed for strengthening the Imperial Government and maintaining the integrity of China, in which it believes the whole Western World is alike concerned. It believes . . . that the present is a very favorable moment for informing Her Majesty's Government of the desire of the United States to have it make on its own part and to lend its powerful support in the effort to obtain from each of the various powers claiming "spheres of interest" in China a declaration substantially to the following effect:

(1) That it will in no wise interfere with any treaty port or any vested interest within any so-called "sphere

[1] From Malloy, *Treaties, Conventions,* etc., I, pp. 249-251.

of interest" or leased territory it may have in China.

(2) That the Chinese treaty tariff of the time being shall apply to all merchandise landed or shipped to all such ports as are within such "spheres of interest" (unless they be "free ports"), no matter to what nationality it may belong, and that duties so leviable shall be collected by the Chinese Government.

(3) That it will levy no higher harbor dues on vessels of another nationality frequenting any port in such "sphere" than shall be levied on vessels of its own nationality and no higher railroad charges over lines built, controlled, or operated within its "sphere" on merchandise belonging to citizens or subjects of other nationalities transported through such "sphere" than shall be levied on similar merchandise belonging to its own nationals transported over equal distances. . . .

B.   HAY'S PROCLAMATION OF THE OPEN DOOR POLICY

Instructions sent *mutatis mutandis* to the United States ambassadors at London, Paris, Berlin, St. Petersburg, and Rome and to the United States Minister at Tokyo, March 20, 1900 [1]

Sir: The ———— Government having accepted the declaration suggested by the United States concerning foreign trade in China, the terms of which I transmitted to you in my instruction No. —— of ————, and like action having been taken by all the various powers having leased territory or so-called "spheres of interest" in the Chinese Empire, as shown by the notes which I herewith transmit to you, you will please inform the government to which you are accredited that the condition originally attached to its acceptance—that all other powers concerned should likewise accept the proposals of the United States—having been complied with, this Government will therefore consider the assent given to it by —— as final and definitive.

You will also transmit to the minister for foreign affairs copies of the present inclosures, and by the same occasion convey to him the expression of the sincere gratification which the President feels at the successful termination of these negotiations, in which he sees proof

[1] Malloy, *op. cit.,* I, p. 260.

of the friendly spirit which animates the various powers interested in the untrammeled development of commerce and industry in the Chinese Empire and a course of vast benefit to the whole commercial world.

I am, etc.,

JOHN HAY

C.   HAY'S FURTHER FORMULATION OF POLICY ON CHINA

Circular telegram to United States representatives at Berlin, London, Paris, Rome, St. Petersburg, Tokyo and Vienna. July 3, 1900.[1]

In this critical posture of affairs in China it is deemed appropriate to define the attitude of the United States as far as present circumstances permit this to be done. We adhere to the policy initiated by us in 1857, of peace with the Chinese nation, of furtherance of lawful commerce, and of protection of lives and property of our citizens by all means guaranteed under extraterritorial treaty rights and by the law of nations. If wrong be done to our citizens we propose to hold the responsible authors to the uttermost accountability. We regard the condition at Pekin as one of virtual anarchy, whereby power and responsibility are practically devolved upon the local provincial authorities. So long as they are not in overt collusion with rebellion and use their power to protect foreign life and property we regard them as representing the Chinese people, with whom we seek to remain in peace and friendship. The purpose of the President is, as it has been heretofore, to act concurrently with the other powers, first, in opening up communication with Pekin and rescuing the American officials, missionaries, and other Americans who are in danger; secondly, in affording all possible protection everywhere in China to American life and property; thirdly, in guarding and protecting all legitimate American interests; and fourthly, in aiding to prevent a spread of the disorders to the other provinces of the Empire and a recurrence of such disasters. It is, of course, too early to forecast the means of attaining this last result, but the policy of the government of the United States is to seek a solution which may bring about permanent safety and peace to China, preserve Chinese

[1] *Foreign Relations of the United States,* 1900, p. 299.

territorial and administrative entity, protect all rights guaranteed to friendly powers by treaty and international law, and safeguard for the world the principle of equal and impartial trade with all parts of the Chinese Empire.

You will communicate the purport of this instruction to the minister for foreign affairs.

HAY.

— 26 —

HAY-PAUNCEFOTE TREATY, NOVEMBER 18, 1901 [1]

Between the Clayton-Bulwer Treaty of 1850 and the end of the century, the United States' need of an isthmian canal had been demonstrated repeatedly, and most dramatically during the war with Spain. Furthermore, American public and official opinion expressed with mounting insistence the conviction that the United States should enjoy exclusive control of the canal. In 1900 Secretary of State John Hay persuaded the British government to negotiate a new treaty which he hoped would satisfy the patriots without affronting Britain. The first effort of Hay and the English ambassador, Lord Pauncefote, was amended by the Senate and in its new form rejected by Britain. A second Hay-Pauncefote treaty contained enough concessions to the burgeoning sense of American power and importance to win Senate approval, and the Foreign office, on second thought, gave its approval. This agreement marks Britain's recognition that the Caribbean area had become an American sphere of influence.

✓   ✓   ✓

The United States of America and His Majesty Edward the Seventh, of the United Kingdom of Great Britain and

[1] From Malloy, *Treaties, Conventions, etc.,* I, pp. 782-784.

Ireland, and of the British Dominions beyond the Seas, King, and Emperor of India, being desirous to facilitate the construction of a ship canal to connect the Atlantic and Pacific Oceans, by whatever route may be considered expedient, and to that end to remove any objection which may arise out of the Convention of the 19th April, 1850, commonly called the Clayton-Bulwer Treaty, to the construction of such canal under the auspices of the Government of the United States, without impairing the "general principle" of neutralization established in Article VIII of that Convention . . . have agreed upon the following Articles:—

ARTICLE I. The High Contracting Parties agree that the present Treaty shall supersede the afore-mentioned Convention of the 19th of April, 1850.

ARTICLE II. It is agreed that the canal may be constructed under the auspices of the Government of the United States, either directly at its own cost, or by gift or loan of money to individuals or Corporations, or through subscription to or purchase of stocks or shares, and that, subject to the provisions of the present Treaty, the said Government shall have and enjoy all the rights incident to such construction, as well as the exclusive right of providing for the regulation and management of the canal.

ARTICLE III. The United States adopts, as the basis of the neutralization of such ship canal, the following Rules, substantially as embodied in the Convention of Constantinople, signed the 28th October, 1888, for the free navigation of the Suez Canal, that is to say:

1. The canal shall be free and open to the vessels of commerce and of war of all nations observing these Rules, on terms of entire equality, so that there shall be no discrimination against any such nation, or its citizens or subjects, in respect of the conditions or charges of traffic, or otherwise. Such conditions and charges of traffic shall be just and equitable.

2. The canal shall never be blockaded, nor shall any right of war be exercised nor any act of hostility be committed within it. The United States, however, shall be at liberty to maintain such military police along the canal as may be necessary to protect it against lawlessness and disorder.

3. Vessels of war of a belligerent shall not revictual nor take any stores in the canal except so far as may be strictly necessary; and the transit of such vessels through the canal shall be effected with the least possible delay. . . .

4. No belligerent shall embark or disembark troops, munitions of war, or warlike materials in the canal, except in case of accidental hindrance of the transit, and in such case the transit shall be resumed with all possible dispatch.

5. The provisions of this Article shall apply to waters adjacent to the canal, within 3 marine miles of either end. . . .

6. The plant, establishments, buildings, and all work necessary to the construction, maintenance, and operation of the canal shall be deemed to be part thereof, for the purpose of this Treaty, and in time of war, as in time of peace, shall enjoy complete immunity from attack or injury by belligerents, and from acts calculated to impair their usefulness as part of the canal.

ARTICLE IV. It is agreed that no change of territorial sovereignty or of international relations of the country or countries traversed by the before-mentioned canal shall affect the general principle of neutralization or the obligation of the High Contracting Parties under the present Treaty. . . .

JOHN HAY
PAUNCEFOTE

— 27 —

PLATT AMENDMENT: TREATY WITH CUBA, MAY 22, 1903[1]

By accepting the Teller amendment to the Cuban resolutions that brought on war with Spain, Congress had

[1] From Malloy, *Treaties, Conventions, etc.,* I, pp. 362-364.

explicitly disclaimed any intention of annexing Cuba; but Cuba's sovereignty was circumscribed by conditions formulated by McKinley's Secretary of War, Elihu Root. Tacked on to an army appropriation bill by Senator Orville H. Platt of Connecticut, these conditions became law in March, 1901, and have been since known as the Platt Amendment. In this way Congress not only defined future relations between the United States and Cuba, but required Cuba to embody the Platt Amendment both in its constitution and in a permanent treaty with the United States. After a period of resistance, Cuba signified its acceptance of the terms of the Platt Amendment by a formal treaty concluded on May 22, 1903. This treaty was abrogated in 1934.

✦   ✦   ✦

ARTICLE I. The Government of Cuba shall never enter into any treaty or other compact with any foreign power or powers which will impair or tend to impair the independence of Cuba, nor in any manner authorize or permit any foreign power or powers to obtain by colonization or for military or naval purposes, or otherwise, lodgment in or control over any portion of said island.

ARTICLE II. The Government of Cuba shall not assume or contract any public debt to pay the interest upon which, and to make reasonable sinking fund provision for the ultimate discharge of which, the ordinary revenues of the Island of Cuba, after defraying the current expenses of the Government, shall be inadequate.

ARTICLE III. The Government of Cuba consents that the United States may exercise the right to intervene for the preservation of Cuban independence, the maintenance of a government adequate for the protection of life, property, and individual liberty, and for discharging the obligations with respect to Cuba imposed by the Treaty of Paris on the United States, now to be assumed and undertaken by the Government of Cuba.

ARTICLE IV. All acts of the United States in Cuba during its military occupancy thereof are ratified and validated, and all lawful rights acquired thereunder shall be maintained and protected.

ARTICLE V. The Government of Cuba will execute, and, as far as necessary, extend the plans already devised, or other plans to be mutually agreed upon, for the sanitation of the cities of the island, to the end that a recurrence of epidemic and infectious diseases may be prevented, thereby assuring protection to the people and commerce of Cuba, as well as to the commerce of the Southern ports of the United States and the people residing therein.

ARTICLE VI. The Island of Pines shall be omitted from the boundaries of Cuba specified in the Constitution, the title thereto being left to future adjustment by treaty.

ARTICLE VII. To enable the United States to maintain the independence of Cuba, and to protect the people thereof, as well as for its own defense, the Government of Cuba will sell or lease to the United States lands necessary for coaling or naval stations, at certain specified points, to be agreed upon with the President of the United States. . . .

— 28 —

ROOSEVELT COROLLARY OF THE MONROE DOCTRINE, DECEMBER 6, 1904 [1]

In 1895 Cleveland's Secretary of State, Richard Olney, had warned Great Britain against intervention in Latin America by vauntingly asserting that the United States was "practically sovereign on this continent" and "practically invulnerable as against any or all other powers." Despite this warning, Great Britain, Germany and Italy sent warships to Venezuela in 1902 to force its dictator,

[1] From Richardson, ed., *Messages and Papers of the Presidents*, X, pp. 831-832.

Cipriano Castro, to honor the claims of his foreign creditors. The episode ended when Castro agreed to arbitrate, but President Theodore Roosevelt continued to ponder its significance. He was certain that Castro deserved to be called to order, but pressure by foreign navies might lead to a violation of the Monroe Doctrine. Roosevelt finally solved the dilemma to his own satisfaction by stating that the United States would assume the policeman's role in the Americas, particularly in the Caribbean area. The policing occasioned considerable intervention in succeeding years, but the property rights of Americans, rather than foreigners, were usually at issue. This pronouncement was embodied in Roosevelt's fourth annual message to Congress.

✓   ✓   ✓

. . . It is not true that the United States feels any land hunger or entertains any projects as regards the other nations of the Western Hemisphere save such as are for their welfare. All that this country desires is to see the neighboring countries stable, orderly, and prosperous. Any country whose people conduct themselves well can count upon our hearty friendship. If a nation shows that it knows how to act with reasonable efficiency and decency in social and political matters, if it keeps order and pays its obligations, it need fear no interference from the United States. Chronic wrongdoing, or an impotence which results in a general loosening of the ties of civilized society, may in America, as elsewhere, ultimately require intervention by some civilized nation, and in the Western Hemisphere the adherence of the United States to the Monroe Doctrine may force the United States, however reluctantly, in flagrant cases of such wrongdoing or impotence, to the exercise of an international police power. If every country washed by the Caribbean Sea would show the progress in stable and just civilization which with the aid of the Platt amendment Cuba has shown since our troops left the island, and which so many of the republics in both Americas are constantly and brilliantly showing, all questions of interference by this Nation with their affairs would be at an end. Our interests and those of our southern neighbors are in reality identical. They have great natural riches, and if within their borders the reign of law and justice obtains, prosperity is sure to come to them. While they thus obey the primary laws of civilized society they may rest assured that they will be treated by us in a spirit of cordial and helpful sympathy. We would interfere with them only in the last resort, and then only if it became evident that their inability or unwillingness to do justice at home and abroad had violated the rights of the United States or had invited foreign aggression to the detriment of the entire body of American nations. It is a mere truism to say that every nation, whether in America or anywhere else, which desires to maintain its freedom, its independence, must ultimately realize that the right of such independence can not be separated from the responsibility of making good use of it. . . .

— 29 →

ALGECIRAS: THE SENATE DISCLAIMER, DECEMBER 12, 1906[1]

Theodore Roosevelt was very conscious that he was head of a newly arrived world power, and he had no hesitation in throwing American influence into the scales of international affairs. Having played a major role in bringing the Russo-Japanese war to an end, he turned his attention to the European crisis of 1905 which grew out of a German challenge to French overlordship in Morocco. Roosevelt sent an American delegation to the

[1] From *United States Statutes at Large*, XXXIV, Part 3, p. 2946.

Algeciras conference of 1906 which dealt with Morocco, and the United States was a signatory to the resulting treaty. Roosevelt felt that his diplomacy had helped to maintain the balance of power in Europe, and his Secretary of State, Elihu Root, loyally maintained that world peace had been preserved by Roosevelt's intercession. The Senate recommended ratification of the Treaty of Algeciras, but added a "disclaimer of political interest" which indicates that the President had plunged more deeply into world affairs than his countrymen.

✓ ✓ ✓

Whereas, in giving its advice and consent to the ratification of the said General Act and Additional Protocol, the Senate of the United States resolved, "as a part of this act of ratification, that the Senate understands that the participation of the United States in the Algeciras Conference, and in the formulation and adoption of the General Act and Protocol which resulted therefrom, was with the sole purpose of preserving and increasing its commerce in Morocco, the protection as to life, liberty and property of its citizens residing or traveling there, and of aiding by its friendly offices and efforts in removing friction and controversy which seemed to menace the peace between the powers signatory with the United States to the Treaty of 1880, all of which are on terms of amity with this government; and without purpose to depart from the traditional American foreign policy which forbids participation by the United States in the settlement of political questions which are entirely European in their scope."

ROOT-TAKAHIRA AGREEMENT, NOVEMBER 30, 1908[1]

This executive agreement was effected through an exchange of notes between Theodore Roosevelt's Secretary of State and Japan's ambassador in Washington. The agreement rendered lip service to the traditional Open Door policy in China, but it paid its respects also to power realities in the Far East. The United States gained some degree of security for the Philippines, which Roosevelt considered an Achilles heel, and the emphasis on the status quo *could be interpreted as American endorsement of Japan's new authority in Manchuria.*

1. It is the wish of the two governments to encourage the free and peaceful development of their commerce on the Pacific Ocean.

2. The policy of both Governments, uninfluenced by any aggressive tendencies, is directed to the maintenance of the existing status quo in the region above mentioned and to the defense of the principle of equal opportunity for commerce and industry in China.

3. They are accordingly firmly resolved reciprocally to respect the territorial possessions belonging to each other in said region.

4. They are also determined to preserve the common interest of all powers in China by supporting by all pacific means at their disposal the independence and integrity of China and the principle of equal opportunity for commerce and industry of all nations in that Empire.

5. Should any event occur threatening the status quo as above described or the principle of equal opportunity as above defined, it remains for the two Governments to

[1] From Malloy, *Treaties, Conventions, etc.,* I, pp. 1045-1047.

communicate with each other in order to arrive at an understanding as to what measures they may consider it useful to take. . . .

— 31 —

TAFT ON DOLLAR DIPLOMACY, DECEMBER 3, 1912[1]

Traditional treaties of "amity and commerce" suggest that diplomacy served to open doors for trade. Early in the 20th century, American diplomats were assigned the more difficult role of promoting foreign loans and investments, and then dealing with defaulters. President Taft thought of dollars as taking the place of bullets, but whether the diplomat was aiding the investor, or the investor furthering policy, the partnership frequently relied on the American marine in the Caribbean. This statement is taken from Taft's fourth annual message to Congress.

To the Senate and House of Representatives:
. . . The diplomacy of the present administration has sought to respond to modern ideas of commercial intercourse. This policy has been characterized as substituting dollars for bullets. It is one that appeals alike to idealistic humanitarian sentiments, to the dictates of sound policy and strategy, and to legitimate commercial aims. It is an effort frankly directed to the increase of American trade upon the axiomatic principle that the Government of the United States shall extend all proper support to every legitimate and beneficial American enterprise abroad. . . .

[1] From *Papers Relating to the Foreign Relations of the United States,* 1912, pp. vii-xii.

In China the policy of encouraging financial investment to enable that country to help itself has had the result of giving new life and practical application to the open-door policy. The consistent purpose of the present administration has been to encourage the use of American capital in the development of China by the promotion of those essential reforms to which China is pledged by treaties with the United States and other powers. The hypothecation to foreign bankers in connection with certain industrial enterprises, such as the Hukuang railways, of the national revenues upon which these reforms depended, led the Department of State early in the administration to demand for American citizens participation in such enterprises, in order that the United States might have equal rights and an equal voice in all questions pertaining to the disposition of the public revenues concerned. The same policy of promoting international accord among the powers having similar treaty rights as ourselves in the matters of reform, which could not be put into practical effect without the common consent of all, was likewise adopted in the case of the loan desired by China for the reform of its currency. . . .

In Central America the aim has been to help such countries as Nicaragua and Honduras to help themselves. They are the immediate beneficiaries. The national benefit to the United States is two-fold. First it is obvious that the Monroe doctrine is more vital in the neighborhood of the Panama Canal and the zone of the Caribbean than anywhere else. There, too, the maintenance of that doctrine falls most heavily upon the United States. It is therefore essential that the countries within that sphere shall be removed from the jeopardy involved by heavy foreign debt and chaotic national finances and from the ever-present dangers of international complications due to disorders at home. Hence the United States has been glad to encourage and support American bankers who were willing to lend a helping hand to the financial rehabilitation of such countries because this financial rehabilitation and the protection of their customshouses from being the prey of would-be dictators would remove at one stroke the menace of foreign creditors and the menace of revolutionary disorder.

The second advantage to the United States is one affecting chiefly all the southern and Gulf ports and the business and industry of the South. The Republics of Central America and the Caribbean possess great natural wealth. They need only a measure of stability and the means of financial regeneration to enter upon an era of peace and prosperity, bring profit and happiness to themselves and at the same time creating conditions sure to lead to a flourishing interchange of trade with this country. . . .

— 32 —

WILSON'S APPEAL FOR NEUTRALITY, AUGUST 19, 1914[1]

Upon the outbreak of World War I, Woodrow Wilson issued the customary proclamation of neutrality setting forth the rights and obligations of nation and citizens as neutrals. In it he strongly enjoined neutrality of action, but conceded that the laws of the United States did not restrict "the free and full expression of sympathies in public and private." However, two weeks later, in a message to the Senate, he felt called upon to dwell on the risks of partisanship even in expression and in thought. In this appeal for neutrality, Wilson already cast the United States in a major role in bringing the world back to peace, though he was later to discover that the United States could not be a peacemaker without being first a belligerent.

✓   ✓   ✓

[1] From U. S. 63rd Congress, 2nd Session, Senate Documents, Vol. 29, No. 566.

My Fellow Countrymen: I suppose that every thoughtful man in America has asked himself, during these last troubled weeks, what influence the European war may exert upon the United States, and I take the liberty of addressing a few words to you in order to point out that it is entirely within our own choice what its effects upon us will be and to urge very earnestly upon you the sort of speech and conduct which will best safeguard the Nation against distress and disaster. . . .

The people of the United States are drawn from many nations, and chiefly from the nations now at war. It is natural and inevitable that there should be the utmost variety of sympathy and desire among them with regard to the issues and circumstances of the conflict. Some will wish one nation, others another, to succeed in the momentous struggle. It will be easy to excite passion and difficult to allay it. Those responsible for exciting it will assume a heavy responsibility, responsibility for no less a thing than that the people of the United States, whose love of their country and whose loyalty to its government should unite them as Americans all, bound in honor and affection to think first of her and her interests, may be divided in camps of hostile opinion, hot against each other, involved in the war itself in impulse and opinion if not in action. . . .

I venture, therefore, my fellow countrymen, to speak a solemn word of warning to you against that deepest, most subtle, most essential breach of neutrality which may spring out of partisanship, out of passionately taking sides. The United States must be neutral in fact as well as in name during these days that are to try men's souls. We must be impartial in thought as well as in action, must put a curb upon our sentiments as well as upon every transaction that might be construed as a preference of one party to the struggle before another.

My thought is of America. I am speaking, I feel sure, the earnest wish and purpose of every thoughtful American that this great country of ours, which is, of course, the first in our thoughts and in our hearts, should show herself in this time of peculiar trial a Nation fit beyond others to exhibit the fine poise of undisturbed judgment, the dignity of self-control, the efficiency of dispassionate action; a Nation that neither sits in judgment upon others nor is disturbed in her own counsels and which keeps herself fit and free to do what is honest and disinterested and truly serviceable for the peace of the world.

Shall we not resolve to put upon ourselves the restraints which will bring to our people the happiness and the great and lasting influence for peace we covet for them?

— 33 —

FIRST *LUSITANIA* NOTE, MAY 13, 1915 [1]

While the United States remained neutral in World War I, President Wilson frequently protested British disregard of traditional American trading rights; but Germany's submarine warfare inspired his sternest warning in 1915 and finally became a major cause of American belligerency. The British liner, Lusitania, *was sunk by a German submarine on May 7, 1915 with the loss of more than a thousand persons of whom 128 were Americans. Wilson's severity in notes of protest soon led to the resignation of his Secretary of State, William Jennings Bryan; but it effected by late summer a degree of restraint in German submarine practices which lasted until February 1, 1917. This note went to Ambassador Gerard in Berlin for communication to the German Minister of Foreign Affairs.*

✓   ✓   ✓

In view of recent acts of the German authorities in violation of American rights on the high seas which culminated in the torpedoing and sinking of the British

[1] From *Papers Relating to the Foreign Relations of the United States*, 1915, Supplement, pp. 393-396.

steamship *Lusitania* on May 7, 1915, by which over 100 American citizens lost their lives, it is clearly wise and desirable that the Government of the United States and the Imperial German Government should come to a clear and full understanding as to the grave situation which has resulted.

The sinking of the British passenger steamer *Falaba* by a German submarine on March 28, through which Leon C. Thrasher, an American citizen, was drowned; the attack on April 28 on the American vessel *Cushing* by a German aeroplane; the torpedoing on May 1 of the American vessel *Gulflight,* by a German submarine, as a result of which two or more American citizens met their death; and, finally, the torpedoing and sinking of the steamship *Lusitania,* constitute a series of events which the Government of the United States has observed with growing concern, distress, and amazement. . . .

The Government of the United States has been apprised that the Imperial German Government considered themselves obliged by the extraordinary circumstances of the present war and the measures adopted by their adversaries in seeking to cut Germany off from all commerce, to adopt methods of retaliation which go much beyond the ordinary methods of warfare at sea, in the proclamation of a war zone from which they have warned neutral ships to keep away. This Government has already taken occasion to inform the Imperial German Government that it can not admit the adoption of such measures or such a warning of danger to operate as in any degree an abbreviation of the rights of American shipmasters or of American citizens bound on lawful errands as passengers on merchant ships of belligerent nationality; and that it must hold the Imperial German Government to a strict accountability for any infringement of those rights, intentional or incidental. It does not understand the Imperial German Government to question those rights. . . .

The Government of the United States, therefore, desires to call the attention of the Imperial German Government with the utmost earnestness to the fact that the objection to their present method of attack against the trade of their enemies lies in the practical impossibility of employing submarines in the destruction of commerce without disregarding those rules of fairness, reason, justice, and humanity which all modern opinion regards as imperative. . . .

American citizens act within their indisputable rights in taking their ships and in traveling wherever their legitimate business calls them upon the high seas, and exercise those rights in what should be the well-justified confidence that their lives will not be endangered by acts done in clear violation of universally acknowledged international obligations, and certainly in the confidence that their own Government will sustain them in the exercise of their rights. . . .

Long acquainted as this Government has been with the character of the Imperial German Government and with the high principles of equity by which they have in the past been actuated and guided, the Government of the United States . . . confidently expects, therefore, that the Imperial German Government will disavow the acts of which the Government of the United States complains, that they will make reparation so far as reparation is possible for injuries which are without measure, and that they will take immediate steps to prevent the recurrence of anything so obviously subversive of the principles of warfare for which the Imperial German Government have in the past so wisely and so firmly contended. . . .

BRYAN

WILSON'S SHIFT ON WAR LOANS, AUGUST 26, 1915 [1]

At the beginning of World War I, President Wilson accepted the dictum of Bryan, his Secretary of State, that "money is the worst of all contrabands because it commands everything else." Consequently, although with no legal warrant, American loans or credits to either belligerent were not officially approved. In the fall of 1914 the ban was removed from credits, and by the summer of 1915 American prosperity depended on war orders which would soon require large-scale American financing. Robert Lansing, who succeeded Bryan at the State Department in June, favored loans to the Allies, and late in August he was relieved to discover that President Wilson was at least neutral, if still sensitive, on the subject. In a matter of weeks an Anglo-French bond issue of $500,-000,000 was floated in the United States. In this note to Lansing, the President repeated the phrasing of the banker's inquiry which for telegraphic purposes referred to the administration as "parties."

✓   ✓   ✓

My dear Mr. Secretary:

My opinion in this matter, compendiously stated, is that we should say that "Parties would take no action either for or against such a transaction," but that this should be orally conveyed, so far as we are concerned, and not put in writing.

I hope this is also your own judgment of the matter.

Faithfully yours,

W. W.

[1] From *Foreign Relations of the United States: The Lansing Papers*, I, p. 144.

WILSON'S WAR MESSAGE, APRIL 2, 1917[1]

Wilson broke off diplomatic relations with Germany when he learned that the Kaiser's government had decided to resume unrestricted submarine warfare against all shipping in the vicinity of the British Isles, France, and Italy. He then turned briefly to the expedient of "armed neutrality," but the sinking of several American merchantmen in March ended the debate in his own mind. The war message he delivered before Congress on April 2 shows that Wilson was concerned with issues beyond American rights at sea and already looked forward to a postwar concert of power which would at last give men freedom, justice, and peace. The vote for war was 373 to 50 in the House of Representatives, 82 to 6 in the Senate.

✓   ✓   ✓

I have called the Congress into extraordinary session because there are serious, very serious, choices of policy to be made, and made immediately, which it was neither right nor constitutionally permissible that I should assume the responsibility of making.

On the third of February last I officially laid before you the extraordinary announcement of the Imperial German Government that on and after the first day of February it was its purpose to put aside all restraints of law or of humanity and use its submarines to sink every vessel that sought to approach either the ports of Great Britain and Ireland or the western coasts of Europe or any of the ports controlled by the enemies of Germany

[1] From U. S. 65th Congress, 1st Session, Senate Documents, Vol. 10, No. 5.

within the Mediterranean. That had seemed to be the object of the German submarine warfare earlier in the war, but since April of last year the Imperial Government had somewhat restrained the commanders of its undersea craft in conformity with its promise then given to us that passenger boats should not be sunk and that due warning would be given to all other vessels which its submarines might seek to destroy, when no resistance was offered or escape attempted. . . . The new policy has swept every restriction aside. Vessels of every kind, whatever their flag, have been ruthlessly sent to the bottom without warning and without thought of help or mercy for those on board. . . .

I was for a little while unable to believe that such things would in fact be done by any government that had hitherto subscribed to the humane practices of civilized nations. . . . I am not now thinking of the loss of property involved, immense and serious as that is, but only of the wanton and wholesale destruction of the lives of non-combatants, men, women, and children, engaged in pursuits which have always, even in the darkest periods of modern history, been deemed innocent and legitimate. Property can be paid for; the lives of peaceful and innocent people cannot be. The present German submarine warfare against commerce is a warfare against mankind.

It is a war against all nations. American ships have been sunk, American lives taken, in ways which it has stirred us very deeply to learn of, but the ships and people of other neutral and friendly nations have been sunk and overwhelmed in the waters in the same way. There has been no discrimination. The challenge is to all mankind. . . .

With a profound sense of the solemn and even tragical character of the step I am taking and of the grave responsibilities which it involves, but in unhesitating obedience to what I deem my constitutional duty, I advise that the Congress declare the recent course of the Imperial German Government to be in fact nothing less than war against the government and people of the United States; that it formally accept the status of belligerent which has thus been thrust upon it; and that it take immediate steps not only to put the country in a more thorough state of defense but also to exert all its power and employ all its resources to bring the Government of the German Empire to terms and end the war. . . .

While we do these things, these deeply momentous things, let us be very clear, and make very clear to all the world what our motives and our objects are. My own thought has not been driven from its habitual and normal course by the unhappy events of the last two months, and I do not believe that the thought of the Nation has been altered or clouded by them. I have exactly the same things in mind now that I had in mind when I addressed the Senate on the twenty-second of January last; the same that I had in mind when I addressed the Congress on the third of February and on the twenty-sixth of February. Our object now, as then, is to vindicate the principles of peace and justice in the life of the world as against selfish and autocratic power and to set up amongst the really free and self-governed peoples of the world such a concert of purpose and of action as will henceforth insure the observance of those principles. Neutrality is no longer feasible or desirable where the peace of the world is involved and the freedom of its peoples, and the menace to that peace and freedom lies in the existence of autocratic governments backed by organized force which is controlled wholly by their will, not by the will of their people. We have seen the last of neutrality in such circumstances. . . .

We have no quarrel with the German people. We have no feeling towards them but one of sympathy and friendship. It was not upon their impulse that their government acted in entering this war. It was not with their previous knowledge or approval. It was a war determined upon as wars used to be determined upon in the old, unhappy days when peoples were nowhere consulted by their rulers and wars were provoked and waged in the interest of dynasties or of little groups of ambitious men who were accustomed to use their fellow men as pawns and tools. . . .

We are accepting this challenge of hostile purpose because we know that in such a Government, following such methods, we can never have a friend. . . . We are glad, now that we see the facts with no veil of false pretense about them, to fight thus for the ultimate peace of the world and for the liberation of its peoples, the German peoples included: for the rights of nations great and small and the privilege of men everywhere to choose their way of life and of obedience. The world must be made safe for democracy. Its peace must be planted upon the tested foundations of political liberty. . . .

It is a distressing and oppressive duty, Gentlemen of the Congress, which I have performed in thus addressing you. There are, it may be, many months of fiery trial and sacrifice ahead of us. It is a fearful thing to lead this great peaceful people into war, into the most terrible and disastrous of all wars, civilization itself seeming to be in the balance. But the right is more precious than peace, and we shall fight for the things which we have always carried nearest our hearts,—for democracy, for the right of those who submit to authority to have a voice in their own Governments, for the rights and liberties of small nations, for a universal dominion of right by such a concert of free peoples as shall bring peace and safety to all nations and make the world itself at last free. To such a task we can dedicate our lives and our fortunes, everything that we are and everything that we have, with the pride of those who know that the day has come when America is privileged to spend her blood and her might for the principles that gave her birth and happiness and the peace which she has treasured. God helping her, she can do no other.

— 36 —

LANSING-ISHII AGREEMENT, NOVEMBER 2, 1917[1]

World War I gave Japan new opportunity in China and early in 1915 her Twenty-One Demands threatened to

[1] United States Relations with China, Department of State Publication 3573, Released August, 1949, p. 437.

turn all of China into a Japanese protectorate. The United States protested strongly, but in 1917 recognized the value of an understanding with Japan since they were now co-belligerents against Germany. A special envoy, Viscount Ishii, propounded the claim that Japan's propinquity to China gave it "paramount interest" there, while Secretary of State Lansing defended China's integrity and the open door. The inclusion of these two positions in a single document was something of a diplomatic triumph. The agreement was formally terminated by an exchange of notes on April 14, 1923, when the Nine-Power Treaty went into effect.

Secretary Lansing to Viscount Ishii,

EXCELLENCY: . . .

The Governments of the United States and Japan recognize that territorial propinquity creates special relations between countries, and, consequently, the Government of the United States recognizes that Japan has special interests in China, particularly in the part to which her possessions are contiguous.

The territorial sovereignty of China, nevertheless, remains unimpaired and the Government of the United States has every confidence in the repeated assurances of the Imperial Japanese Government that while geographical position gives Japan such special interests they have no desire to discriminate against the trade of other nations or to disregard the commercial rights heretofore granted by China in treaties with other powers.

The Governments of the United States and Japan deny that they have any purpose to infringe in any way the independence or territorial integrity of China and they declare, furthermore, that they always adhere to the principle of the so-called "open-door" or equal opportunity for commerce and industry in China.

Moreover, they mutually declare that they are opposed to the acquisition by any Government of any special rights or privileges that would affect the independence or territorial integrity of China or that would deny to the subjects or citizens of any country the full enjoyment of equal opportunity in the commerce and industry of China. . . .

ROBERT LANSING

— 37 —

THE FOURTEEN POINTS, JANUARY 8, 1918[1]

Midway between the American declaration of war on Germany and the armistice, President Wilson proclaimed the famous Fourteen Points as the American program of peace in an address to Congress. His general purpose was to list concrete objectives in harmony with his vision of a better world, and to influence and mobilize American and Allied opinion in favor of a new way of international life. More specifically Wilson sought to dissuade the new Bolshevik government in Russia from concluding a separate peace with Germany, and to shorten the war by assuring the Germans that they could expect an honorable peace.

Gentlemen of the Congress: . . .

We entered this war because violations of right had occurred which touched us to the quick and made the life of our own people impossible unless they were corrected and the world secured once for all against their recurrence. What we demand in this war, therefore, is nothing peculiar to ourselves. It is that the world be made fit and safe to live in; and particularly that it be made safe for every peace-loving nation which, like our own, wishes to live its own life, determine its own institu-

[1] From U. S. 65th Congress, 2nd Session, House Documents, Vol. 113, No. 765.

tions, be assured of justice and fair dealing by the other peoples of the world as against force and selfish aggression. All the peoples of the world are in effect partners in this interest, and for our own part we see very clearly that unless justice be done to others it will not be done to us. The program of the world's peace, therefore, is our program; and that program, the only possible program, as we see it, is this:

I. Open covenants of peace, openly arrived at, after which there shall be no private international understandings of any kind but diplomacy shall proceed always frankly and in the public view.

II. Absolute freedom of navigation upon the seas, outside territorial waters, alike in peace and in war, except as the seas may be closed in whole or in part by international action for the enforcement of international covenants.

III. The removal, so far as possible, of all economic barriers and the establishment of an equality of trade conditions among all the nations consenting to the peace and associating themselves for its maintenance.

IV. Adequate guarantees given and taken that national armaments will be reduced to the lowest point consistent with domestic safety.

V. A free, open-minded, and absolutely impartial adjustment of all colonial claims, based upon a strict observance of the principle that in determining all such questions of sovereignty the interests of the populations concerned must have equal weight with the equitable claims of the government whose title is to be determined.

VI. The evacuation of all Russian territory and such a settlement of all questions affecting Russia as will secure the best and freest cooperation of the other nations of the world in obtaining for her an unhampered and unembarrassed opportunity for the independent determination of her own political development and national policy and assure her of a sincere welcome into the society of free nations under institutions of her own choosing. . . .

VII. Belgium, the whole world will agree, must be evacuated and restored, without any attempt to limit the sovereignty which she enjoys in common with all other free nations. . . .

VIII. All French territory should be freed and the invaded portions restored, and the wrong done to France by Prussia in 1871 in the matter of Alsace-Lorraine, which has unsettled the peace of the world for nearly fifty years, should be righted. . . .

IX. A readjustment of the frontiers of Italy should be effected along clearly recognizable lines of nationality.

X. The peoples of Austria-Hungary, whose place among the nations we wish to see safeguarded and assured, should be accorded the freest opportunity of autonomous development.

XI. Rumania, Serbia, and Montenegro should be evacuated, occupied territories restored; Serbia accorded free and secure access to the sea. . . .

XII. The Turkish portions of the present Ottoman Empire should be assured a secure sovereignty, but the other nationalities which are now under Turkish rule should be assured an undoubted security of life and an absolutely unmolested opportunity of autonomous development, and the Dardanelles should be permanently opened as a free passage to the ships and commerce of all nations under international guarantees.

XIII. An independent Polish state should be erected which should include the territories inhabited by indisputably Polish populations, which should be assured a free and secure access to the sea, and whose political and economic independence and territorial integrity should be guaranteed by international covenant.

XIV. A general association of nations must be formed under specific covenants for the purpose of affording mutual guarantees of political independence and territorial integrity to great and small states alike. . . .

For such arrangements and covenants we are willing to fight and to continue to fight until they are achieved; but only because we wish the right to prevail and desire a just and stable peace such as can be secured only by removing the chief provocations to war, which this program does remove. We have no jealousy of German greatness, and there is nothing in this program that impairs it. . . .

We have spoken now, surely, in terms too concrete to admit of any further doubt or question. An evident principle runs through the whole program I have outlined. It is the principle of justice to all peoples and nationalities, and their right to live on equal terms of liberty and safety with one another, whether they be strong or weak. Unless this principle be made its foundation no part of the structure of international justice can stand. The people of the United States could act upon no other principle; and to the vindication of this principle they are ready to devote their lives, their honor, and everything that they possess. The moral climax of this the culminating and final war for human liberty has come, and they are ready to put their own strength, their own highest purpose, their own integrity and devotion to the test.

— 38 —

WILSON'S DEFENSE
OF THE LEAGUE,
AUGUST 19, 1919[1]

President Wilson's central purpose at the peace conference in Paris was also his major triumph: the drafting and adoption of the League of Nations Covenant and its inclusion in the treaties made with each enemy state. Wilson was chairman of a commission which drew up the Covenant on the basis of several preliminary drafts in the first two weeks in February, 1919. Returning to Washington to sign bills late in February, Wilson discussed the Covenant with the foreign affairs committees of both Houses of Congress, and learned that opposition to membership in the League was already being organized. Back in Paris Wilson reconvened his commission and persuaded it to incorporate several changes designed to meet Ameri-

[1] From U. S. 66th Congress, 1st Session, Senate Document 106, pp. 499-503.

can criticism. The Treaty of Versailles with which was
incorporated the League Covenant was laid before the
Senate on July 10. This statement was made by the
President at a meeting of the Senate Committee on For-
eign Relations whose new chairman, Henry Cabot Lodge,
was to play a key role in defeating the League in the
Senate.

Mr. Chairman: . . .

Nothing, I am led to believe, stands in the way of
ratification of the treaty except certain doubts with regard to the meaning and implication of certain articles
of the Covenant of the League of Nations; and I must
frankly say that I am unable to understand why such
doubts should be entertained. You will recall that when
I had the pleasure of a conference with your committee
and with the committee of the House of Representatives
on Foreign Affairs at the White House in March last the
questions now most frequently asked about the League
of Nations were all canvassed with a view to their immediate clarification. The Covenant of the League was
then in its first draft and subject to revision. It was
pointed out that no express recognition was given to the
Monroe Doctrine; that it was not expressly provided that
the League should have no authority to act or to express
a judgment on matters of domestic policy; that the right
to withdraw from the League was not expressly recognized; and that the constitutional right of the Congress to
determine all questions of peace and war was not sufficiently safeguarded. On my return to Paris all these matters were taken up again by the Commission on the
League of Nations, and every suggestion of the United
States was accepted. . . .

The Monroe Doctrine is expressly mentioned as an
understanding which is in no way to be impaired or interfered with by anything contained in the Covenant. . . .

With regard to domestic questions Article 16 of the
Covenant expressly provides that, if in case of any dispute
arising between members of the League the matter involved is claimed by one of the parties "and is found by
the council to arise out of a matter which by international law is solely within the domestic jurisdiction of

that party, the council shall so report, and shall make no recommendation as to its settlement." The United States was by no means the only government interested in the explicit adoption of this provision, and there is no doubt in the mind of any authoritative student of international law that such matters as immigration, tariffs, and naturalization are incontestably domestic questions with which no international body could deal. . . .

The right of any soveregn State to withdraw had been taken for granted, but no objection was made to making it explicit. . . .

Article X is in no respect of doubtful meaning when read in the light of the Covenant as a whole. The Council of the League can only "advise upon" the means by which the obligations of that great article are to be given effect to. Unless the United States is a party to the policy or action in question, her own affirmative vote in the council is necessary before any advice can be given, for a unanimous vote of the council is required. If she is a party, the trouble is hers anyhow. And the unanimous vote of the council is only advice in any case. Each Government is free to reject it if it pleases. Nothing could have been made more clear to the conference than the right of our Congress under our Constitution to exercise its independent judgment in all matters of peace and war. No attempt was made to question or limit that right. The United States will, indeed, undertake under Article X to "respect and preserve as against external aggression the territorial integrity and existing political independence of all members of the League," and that engagement constitutes a very grave and solemn moral obligation. But it is a moral, not a legal, obligation, and leaves our Congress absolutely free to put its own interpretation upon it in all cases that call for action. It is binding in conscience only, not in law.

Article X seems to me to constitute the very backbone of the whole Covenant. Without it the League would be hardly more than an influential debating society.

It has several times been suggested, in public debate and in private conference, that interpretations of the sense in which the United States accepts the engagements of the Covenant should be embodied in the instrument of ratification. There can be no reasonable objection to such interpretations accompanying the act of ratification provided they do not form a part of the formal ratification itself. . . . But if such interpretations should constitute a part of the formal resolution of ratification, long delays would be the inevitable consequence, inasmuch as all the many Governments concerned would have to accept, in effect, the language of the Senate as the language of the treaty before ratification would be complete. . . .

— 39 —

THE WASHINGTON CONFERENCE, 1921-1922

The inspiration for the Washington Conference came from a Congressional resolution which proposed that the United States bring the current naval armaments race to an end by agreement with Great Britain and Japan. Diplomatic soundings were favorable, and the State Department sent out invitations to a nine-power conference to deal with Far Eastern questions as well as with naval limitation. Twelve weeks of deliberations under the skillful chairmanship of Secretary of State Charles Evans Hughes resulted in agreement on three major treaties. The four-power pact (A) supplanted the Anglo-Japanese treaty of alliance whose renewal, now due, was opposed by British dominions and the United States. In recommending ratification of the four-power treaty, the Senate added the reservation that the United States was making no commitment to carry out its terms by action of any kind. In the treaty on naval limitation (B), Great Britain accepted parity with the United States, and Japan inferiority, in the 5-5-3 ratio in capital ships, the naval race was suspended for ten years, and the three powers undertook to build no new fortifications on their west Pacific

*islands. In the nine-power treaty (C) the United States
for the first time obtained formal international agreement
on its traditional Open Door policy in China. The im-
permanence of these agreements became clear later, but
the conference was hailed at the time for its effective use
of discussion and consent to the end of international understanding.*

✓   ✓   ✓

A. FOUR-POWER TREATY ON PACIFIC POSSESSIONS, DECEMBER 13, 1921 [1]

The United States of America, the British Empire,
France and Japan, with a view to the preservation of the
general peace and the maintenance of their rights in relation to their insular possessions and insular dominions
in the region of the Pacific Ocean . . . have agreed as
follows:

I. The High Contracting Parties agree as between themselves to respect their rights in relation to their insular
possessions and insular dominions in the region of the
Pacific Ocean. If there should develop between any of
the High Contracting Parties a controversy arising out
of any Pacific question and involving their said rights
which is not satisfactorily settled by diplomacy and is
likely to affect the harmonious accord now happily subsisting between them, they shall invite the other High
Contracting Parties to a joint conference to which the
whole subject will be referred for consideration and adjustment.

II. If the said rights are threatened by the aggressive
action of any other Power, the High Contracting Parties
shall communicate with one another fully and frankly in
order to arrive at an understanding as to the most efficient measures to be taken, jointly or separately, to meet
the exigencies of the particular situation. . . .

IV. This Treaty . . . shall take effect on the deposit
of ratifications, which shall take place at Washington,
and thereupon the agreement between Great Britain and
Japan which was concluded at London on July 13, 1911,
shall terminate. . . .

[1] From *Statutes at Large of the United States,* XLIII, Pt. 2, pp.
1646-1650.

B.   FIVE-POWER TREATY ON NAVAL LIMITATION, FEBRUARY 6, 1922 [1]

The United States of America, the British Empire, France, Italy and Japan;

Desiring to contribute to the general peace and to reduce the burdens of competition in armaments . . . have agreed as follows:

CHAPTER I.

ARTICLE I. The Contracting Powers agree to limit their respective naval armament as provided in the present Treaty.

ARTICLE II. The Contracting Parties may retain respectively the capital ships which are specified in Chapter II, Part 1 . . . All other capital ships, built or building, of the United States, the British Empire and Japan shall be disposed of. . . .

ARTICLE III. The Contracting Parties shall abandon their respective capital ship building programs, and no new capital ships shall be constructed or acquired by any of the Contracting Powers except replacement tonnage. . . .

ARTICLE IV. The total capital ship replacement tonnage of each of the Contracting Powers shall not exceed in standard displacement, for the United States 525,000 tons; for the British Empire 525,000 tons; for France 175,000 tons; for Italy 175,000 tons; for Japan 315,000 tons.

ARTICLE V. No capital ship exceeding 35,000 tons standard displacement shall be acquired by or constructed by, for or within the jurisdiction of any of the Contracting Powers.

ARTICLE VI. No capital ship of any of the Contracting Powers shall carry a gun with a calibre in excess of 16 inches.

ARTICLE VII. The total tonnage for aircraft carriers of each of the Contracting Parties shall not exceed in standard displacement for the United States 135,000 tons; for the British Empire 135,000 tons; for France 60,000 tons; for Italy 60,000 tons; for Japan 81,000 tons. . . .

[1] *Statutes at Large of the United States,* XLIII, Pt. 2, p. 1655-1685.

ARTICLE XIX. The United States, the British Empire and Japan agree that the status quo at the time of the signing of the present Treaty with regard to fortifications and naval bases, shall be maintained in their respective territories and possessions specified hereunder:

1. The insular possessions which the United States now holds or may hereafter acquire in the Pacific Ocean, except (a) those adjacent to the coast of the United States, Alaska and the Panama Canal Zone, not including the Aleutian Islands, and (b) the Hawaiian Islands;

2. Hongkong and the insular possessions which the British Empire now holds or may hereafter acquire in the Pacific Ocean east of the meridian of 110° east longitude, except (a) those adjacent to the coast of Canada, (b) the Commonwealth of Australia and its Territories and (c) New Zealand;

3. The following insular territories and possessions of Japan in the Pacific Ocean, to wit: the Kurile Islands, the Bonin Islands, Amami-Oshima, the Loochoo Islands, Formosa and the Pescadores, and any insular territories or possessions in the Pacific Ocean which Japan may hereafter acquire. . . .

C. NINE-POWER TREATY ON RELATIONS WITH CHINA, FEBRUARY 6, 1922 [1]

The United States of America, Belgium, the British Empire, China, France, Italy, Japan, the Netherlands and Portugal:

Desiring to adopt a policy designed to stabilize conditions in the Far East, to safeguard the rights and interests of China, and to promote intercourse between China and the other Powers upon the basis of equality of opportunity. . . . have agreed as follows:

I. The Contracting Powers, other than China, agree:

(1) To respect the sovereignty, the independence, and the territorial and administrative integrity of China.

(2) To provide the fullest and most unembarrassed op-

[1] *Statutes at Large of the United States*, XLIV, Pt. 3, pp. 2113-2121.

portunity to China to develop and maintain for herself an effective and stable government.

(3) To use their influence for the purpose of effectually establishing and maintaining the principle of equal opportunity for the commerce and industry of all nations throughout the territory of China;

(4) To refrain from taking advantage of conditions in China in order to seek special rights or privileges which would abridge the rights of subjects or citizens of friendly States, and from countenancing action inimical to the security of such States.

II. The Contracting Powers agree not to enter into any treaty, agreement, arrangement, or understanding, either with one another, or, individually or collectively, with any Power or Powers, which would infringe or impair the principles stated in Article I.

III. With a view to applying more effectually the principles of the Open Door or equality of opportunity in China for the trade and industry of all nations, the Contracting Powers, other than China, agree that they will not seek nor support their respective nationals, in seeking—

(a) any arrangement which might purport to establish in favor of their interests any general superiority of rights with respect to commercial or economic development in any designated region of China.

(b) any such monopoly or preference as would deprive the nationals of any other Power of the right of undertaking any legitimate trade or industry in China . . .

China undertakes to be guided by the principles stated in the foregoing stipulations of this Article in dealing with applications for economic rights and privileges from Governments and nationals of all foreign countries, whether parties to the present Treaty or not. . . .

JAPANESE EXCLUSION, MAY 26, 1924[1]

California succeeded in its campaign for legislation against the immigration of Chinese coolies. Its subsequent attempts to cut off the flow of Japanese laborers resulted in a "Gentleman's Agreement," concluded by President Roosevelt in 1907, by which the Japanese government refused passports to emigrants wishing to enter the United States. Although this agreement continued in effect and served its purpose, the Immigration Act of 1924 totally excluded the Japanese and other Oriental peoples. President Coolidge and Secretary of State Hughes had tried to change this discriminatory provision of the bill, but failed. In signing the bill into law, Coolidge made the statement printed here. The Act has been described as a needless affront to Japan.

✓ ✓ ✓

In signing this Bill, which in its main features I heartily approve, I regret the impossibility of severing from it the exclusion provision which, in the light of existing law, affects especially the Japanese. . . . It should be noted that the Bill excepts from the exclusion provision governments officials, those coming to this country as tourists or temporarily for business or pleasure, those in transit, seamen, those already resident here and returning from temporary absences, professors, ministers of religion, students and those who enter solely to carry on trade in pursuance of existing treaty provisions. But we have had for many years an understanding with Japan by which the Japanese Government has voluntarily undertaken to prevent the emigration of laborers to the United

[1] From *Foreign Relations of the United States*, 1924, II, p. 396.

States, and in view of this historic relation and of the feeling which inspired it, it would have been much better in my judgment, and more effective in the actual control of immigration, if we had continued to invite the co-operation which Japan was ready to give and had thus avoided creating any ground for misapprehension by an unnecessary statutory enactment. . . . If the exclusion provision stood alone I should disapprove it without hesitation, if sought in this way at this time. But this Bill is a comprehensive measure dealing with the whole subject of immigration and setting up the necessary administrative machinery. The present Quota Act, of 1921, will terminate on June 30th next. It is of great importance that a comprehensive measure take its place . . . I must therefore consider the Bill as a whole, and the imperative need of the country for legislation of this general character. For this reason the Bill is approved.

CALVIN COOLIDGE

— 41 —

KELLOGG-BRIAND PACT, AUGUST 27, 1928[1]

The first Hague Peace Conference of 1899 provided for the institution of a Permanent Court of Arbitration, and with this encouragement the State Department under Theodore Roosevelt, Wilson, and Coolidge negotiated an impressive number of treaties of arbitration or conciliation with friendly nations. However, the approach was piecemeal, and a few loopholes were carefully concealed in each treaty. Both deficiencies seemed handsomely corrected by the Pact of Paris, or Kellogg-Briand Pact, which provided for the general renunciation of war. The treaty

[1] From *Foreign Relations of the United States, 1928,* I, pp. 153-156.

was ceremonially signed in Paris on August 27, 1928, and finally adhered to by some sixty sovereign states, including all the aggressors of the following decade. In the Senate the treaty came within one vote of unanimous approval. Aristide Briand was the French Foreign Minister; Frank B. Kellogg, the American Secretary of State.

↗   ↗   ↗

ARTICLE 1. The High Contracting Parties solemnly declare in the names of their respective peoples that they condemn recourse to war for the solution of international controversies, and renounce it as an instrument of national policy in their relations with one another.

ARTICLE 2. The High Contracting Parties agree that the settlement or solution of all disputes or conflicts of whatever nature or of whatever origin they may be, which may arise among them, shall never be sought except by pacific means. . . .

— 42 —

STIMSON ON THE RECOGNITION OF NEW GOVERNMENTS, FEBRUARY 6, 1931[1]

Henry L. Stimson, Secretary of State from 1929 to 1933, made this statement on United States recognition policy in a speech before the Council on Foreign Relations, New York, early in 1931. Although it is clear that Mr. Stimson considered President Wilson's refusal to recognize Latin American governments he did not ap-

[1] From Walter Lippmann and William O. Scroggs, eds., *The United States in World Affairs, 1931* (New York, 1932) pp. 332-334.

prove as aberrational, he himself withheld recognition from the regime which had been "in de facto *possession" of Russia since 1917.*

✔   ✔   ✔

. . . The practice of this country as to the recognition of new governments has been substantially uniform from the days of the administration of Secretary of State Jefferson in 1792 to the days of Secretary of State Bryan in 1913. . . . This general policy, as thus observed, was to base the act of recognition not upon the question of the constitutional legitimacy of the new government but upon its *de facto* capacity to fulfill its obligations as a member of the family of nations. This country recognized the right of other nations to regulate their own internal affairs of government and disclaimed any attempt to base its recognition upon the correctness of their constitutional action. . . .

The particular considerations upon which our action was regularly based were well stated by Mr. Adee, long the trusted Assistant Secretary of State of this Government, as follows:

> Ever since the American Revolution entrance upon diplomatic intercourse with foreign states has been *de facto,* dependent upon the existence of three conditions of fact: the control of the administrative machinery of the state; the general acquiescence of its people; and the ability and willingness of their governments to discharge international and conventional obligations. The form of government has not been a conditional factor in such recognition; in other words, the *de jure* element of legitimacy of title has been left aside.

With the advent of President Wilson's administration this policy of over a century was radically departed from in respect to the Republic of Mexico, and, by a public declaration on March 11, 1913, it was announced that

> Cooperation (with our sister republics) is possible only when supported at every turn by the orderly processes of just government based upon law, not upon arbitrary or irregular force. We hold . . . that just government rests always upon the consent of the governed, and that there can be no freedom without

order based upon law and upon the public conscience
and approval. We shall look to make these principles
the bases of mutual intercourse, respect and helpful-
ness between our sister republics and ourselves.

The present administration has declined to follow the
policy of Mr. Wilson and has followed consistently the
former practice of this government since the days of
Jefferson. As soon as it was reported to us, through our
diplomatic representatives, that the new governments of
Bolivia, Peru, Argentina, Brazil, and Panama were in
control of the administrative machinery of the state,
with the apparent general acquiescence of their people,
and that they were willing and apparently able to discharge their international and conventional obligations
they were recognized by our government. . . .

— 43 —

THE HOOVER MORATORIUM, JUNE 20, 1931[1]

*In the 1920's Great Britain and France could pay off
their war debts to the United States so long as Germany
paid them reparations, and Germany was able to make
reparations payments so long as Americans invested in
German industry and bought German bonds. This merry-
go-round of high finance was jeopardized in 1928 when
American investors turned gaily to their home market.
German reparations were drastically scaled down by the
Young Plan of 1929, but the stock market crash, the
paralyzing Smoot-Hawley tariff act, and the deepening
depression threatened the whole shaky structure of Eu-*

---

[1] From Lippman and Scroggs, eds., *The United States in World
Affairs, 1931*, pp. 336-339.

*ropean finance by the spring of 1931. President Hoover
was convinced that a year's suspension of all inter-gov-
ernmental payments would contribute to recovery and
his proposal was approved by Congress and other governments. Hoover made his proposal public in the hope of
stopping the panic that was overtaking Germany's creditors at home and abroad. His statement had a tranquil-
lizing effect, but the moratorium in fact marked the end
of virtually all payments on either reparations or war
debts.*

ᕀ   ᕀ   ᕀ

The American government proposes the postponement
during one year of all payments on intergovernmental
debts, reparations and relief debts, both principal and
interest, of course not including obligations of governments held by private parties. Subject to confirmation
by Congress, the American government will postpone all
payments upon the debts of foreign governments to the
American government payable during the fiscal year
beginning July 1 next, conditional on a like postponement for one year of all payments on intergovernmental
debts owing the important creditor powers. . . .

The world-wide depression has affected the countries
of Europe more severely than our own. Some of these
countries are feeling to a serious extent the drain of this
depression on national economy. The fabric of intergovernmental debts, supportable in normal times, weighs
heavily in the midst of this depression. . . .

Authority of the President to deal with this problem
is limited, as this action must be supported by the Congress. It has been assured the cordial support of leading
members of both parties in the Senate and the House.
The essence of this proposition is to give time to permit
debtor governments to recover their national prosperity.
I am suggesting to the American people that they be wise
creditors in their own interest and be good neighbors.

I wish to take this occasion also to frankly state my
views upon our relations to German reparations and the
debts owed to us by the Allied governments of Europe. . . .

I do not approve in any remote sense of the cancella-
tion of the debts to us. World confidence would not be

enhanced by such action. None of our debtor nations has ever suggested it. But as the basis of the settlement of these debts was the capacity under normal conditions of the debtor to pay, we should be consistent with our own policies and principles if we take into account the abnormal situation now existing in the world. I am sure the American people have no desire to attempt to extract any sum beyond the capacity of any debtor to pay, and it is our view that broad vision requires that our government should recognize the situation as it exists. . . .

— 44 —

THE STIMSON DOCTRINE, JANUARY 7, 1932[1]

Japan's invasion of Manchuria in September, 1931, violated self-denying provisions of both the Nine-Power Treaty of 1922 and the Kellogg-Briand Pact which Japan and the United States had signed, as well as obligations of the League of Nations. China's appeals to the United States and the League resulted in protests to Japan which were ignored. President Hoover and Secretary of State Stimson were agreed that Japan's action deserved a rejoinder stronger than words but Hoover ruled out force or even economic pressures. The resulting policy, known as the Stimson or the Hoover-Stimson doctrine, ruled out recognition by the United States of any change brought about in violation of international agreements. This was stated in identical notes sent to Japan and China. Great Britain and France were unwilling to subscribe to the new doctrine, but the Assembly of the League endorsed it two months later, without increasing its deterrent effect.

✓   ✓   ✓

[1] From *United States Relations with China,* Department of State Publication 3573, Far Eastern Series 30, pp. 446-447.

With the recent military operations about Chinchow, the last remaining administrative authority of the Government of the Chinese Republic in South Manchuria, as it existed prior to September 18th, 1931, has been destroyed. The American Government continues confident that the work of the neutral commission recently authorized by the Council of the League of Nations will facilitate an ultimate solution of the difficulties now existing between China and Japan. But in view of the present situation and of its own rights and obligations therein, the American Government deems it to be its duty to notify both the Imperial Japanese Government and the Government of the Chinese Republic that it cannot admit the legality of any situation *de facto* nor does it intend to recognize any treaty or agreement entered in to between those Governments, or agents thereof, which may impair the treaty rights of the United States or its citizens in China, including those which relate to the sovereignty, the independence, or the territorial and administrative integrity of the Republic of China, or to the international policy relative to China, commonly known as the open door policy; and that it does not intend to recognize any situation, treaty or agreement which may be brought about by means contrary to the covenants and obligations of the Pact of Paris of August 27, 1928, to which Treaty both China and Japan, as well as the United States, are parties.

— 45 —

THE JOHNSON ACT, APRIL 13, 1934[1]

The United States became the world's leading banker during the first World War, but as a creditor nation it

[1] *The Statutes at Large of the United States,* XLVIII, Pt. I, p. 574.

made the repayment of loans difficult by constantly ex-
porting more goods than it imported. The Smoot-Hawley
Tariff Act of 1930 further reduced the ability of foreign
nations to obtain dollars by trade, and the world-wide
depression then caused widespread default of public
debtors following the one-year Hoover moratorium. By
the end of 1933 war debts owed the United States, in-
cluding arrears, totalled more than eleven billion dollars.
Senator Hiram Johnson, the California isolationist, in-
troduced a bill aimed at foreign defaulters, whether will-
ful or involuntary, which further circumscribed the United
States' role as world banker.

✓   ✓   ✓

An act to prohibit financial transactions with any foreign government in default on its obligations to the
United States.

Be it enacted by the Senate and House of Representa-
tives of the United States in Congress assembled, That
hereafter it shall be unlawful within the United States or
any place subject to the jurisdiction of the United States
for any person to purchase or sell the bonds, securities,
or other obligations of, any foreign government or political subdivision thereof or any organization or association
acting for or on behalf of a foreign government or political subdivision thereof, issued after the passage of this
Act, or to make any loan to such foreign government,
political subdivision, organization, or association, except
a renewal or adjustment of existing indebtedness, while
such government, political subdivision, organization, or
association, is in default in the payment of its obligations,
or any part thereof, to the Government of the United
States. Any person violating the provisions of this Act
shall upon conviction thereof be fined not more than
$10,000 or imprisoned for not more than five years, or
both. . . .

46

THE TRADE AGREEMENTS ACT, JUNE 12, 1934[1]

As Congressman and Senator, Cordell Hull had long been a devoted advocate of lower tariffs but he was backing a losing cause between 1921 and 1933. The Trade Agreements Act he sponsored as Secretary of State reversed the upward trend, and the agreements he negotiated lowered our tariff wall so gradually that there was little outcry from American producers, and Congress periodically extended the arrangement. The other side of that coin was that the program increased exports more than imports, and so widened the trade gap and increased the dollar shortage. Mr. Hull believed that freer trade would lessen the likelihood of war, but he picked an unfortunate decade for the demonstration. President Roosevelt signed the Act on June 12, 1934.

✓ ✓ ✓

What Was the Trade Agreements Act?

First of all, the Trade Agreements Act was an amendment to the Smoot-Hawley Act. It was immaterial, however, whether the Trade Agreements Act was a separate Act or an amendment to an Act. The point was that it was to be fully effective and independently operated just as if it were a separate enactment. Actually it would have been folly to go to Congress and ask that the Smoot-Hawley Act be repealed or its rates reduced by Congress. This had been the old system; and, with the exception of the Underwood Act in 1913, it always resulted in higher tariffs because the special interests enriched by high

[1] From *The Memoirs of Cordell Hull* (New York, 1948), I, pp. 358-365. Copyright of The Macmillan Company, N. Y.

tariffs went to their respective Congressmen and insisted on higher rates. . . .

We therefore started with the Smoot-Hawley tariff rates as the upper limit. The President was now authorized to enter into trade agreements with other countries. These would go into effect without the need for Senate approval or Congressional action. In negotiating such agreements, he was authorized to increase or decrease any of the Smoot-Hawley rates by as much as 50 per cent in return for adequate trade concessions from another country. He could therefore cut in half all existing rates; but we had made it clear that we did not for a moment contemplate such drastic, horizontal action . . . The purpose of the Act was stated to be to improve our exports. . . .

The Trade Agreements Act in itself thus was simple. Basically it contained three main points: Agreements could be negotiated without their having to be submitted to the Senate. Tariffs could be reduced by as much as one-half, but only if we gained corresponding concessions from other countries. Reductions applied to all countries that did not discriminate against us. . . .

The basic approach to the problem of peace is the ordering of the world's economic life so that the masses of the people can work and live in reasonable comfort . . .

And this cannot happen in a world of extreme economic barriers, political hostility, and recurring wars.

The principles underlying the trade agreements program are therefore an indispensable cornerstone for the edifice of peace. . . .

47

DECLARATION OF PRINCIPLES OF INTER-AMERICAN SOLIDARITY AND COOPERATION, DECEMBER 21, 1936[1]

The Inter-American Conference which met at Buenos Aires late in 1936 was said to have "continentalized the Monroe Doctrine," since threats to the peace of America were then and there recognized to be matters of common concern. The United States was aware of the possibility that such a threat might grow out of the penetration or subversion of a Latin American state by Germany or Italy. The sister republics, however, thought it prudent to commit the United States again to the policy of non-intervention it had agreed to at the Montevideo conference in 1933.

1. That the American Nations, true to their republican institutions, proclaim their absolute juridical liberty, their unqualified respect for their respective sovereignties and the existence of a common democracy throughout America;

2. That every act susceptible of disturbing the peace of America affects each and every one of them, and justifies the initiation of the procedure of consultation provided for in the Convention for the Maintenance, Preservation and Reestablishment of Peace, signed at this Conference; and

3. That the following principles are accepted by the American community of Nations:

[1] From *Peace and War,* Department of State Publication 1983, pp. 352-353.

(a) Proscription of territorial conquest and that, in consequence, no acquisition made through violence shall be recognized;

(b) Intervention by one State in the internal or external affairs of another State is condemned;

(c) Forcible collection of pecuniary debts is illegal; and

(d) Any difference or dispute between the American nations, whatever its nature or origin, shall be settled by the methods of conciliation, or unrestricted arbitration, or through operation of international justice.

— 48 —

NEUTRALITY ACT, MAY 1, 1937[1]

The Senate committee set up to investigate the munitions industry in 1934 furnished an isolationist Congress with the assumptions which underlay the neutrality legislation of 1935-1939. Under the chairmanship of Senator Nye of North Dakota, the committee conducted hearings which developed the theme that the United States had been drawn into World War I to save the bankers and armaments-makers. The conclusion was that, if the United States avoided economic ties with belligerents, it need never go to war again. The Acts of 1935 and 1936 had limited tenure, but that of 1937, given below, set no time limit on its basic provisions.

The Act denied American citizens the traditional neutral rights of selling or transporting munitions or making loans to belligerents or nations engaged in civil war, and traveling on belligerent ships. Section 2 of the Act, omitted here, was a limited "cash-and-carry" provision which

[1] From *United States Statutes at Large*, 50, Pt. I, pp. 121-128.

was extended to munitions after the outbreak of World War II.

✓   ✓   ✓

Section 1. (a) Whenever the President shall find that there exists a state of war between, or among, two or more foreign states, the President shall proclaim such fact, and it shall thereafter be unlawful to export, or attempt to export, or cause to be exported, arms, ammunition, or implements of war from any place in the United States to any belligerent state named in such proclamation, or to any neutral state for transshipment to, or for the use of, any such belligerent state. . . .

(c) Whenever the President shall find that a state of civil strife exists in a foreign state and that such civil strife is of a magnitude or is being conducted under such conditions that the export of arms, ammunition, or implements of war from the United States to such foreign state would threaten or endanger the peace of the United States, the President shall proclaim such fact, and it shall thereafter be unlawful to export, or attempt to export, or cause to be exported, arms, ammunition, or implements of war from any place in the United States to such foreign state, or to any neutral state for transshipment to, or for the use of, such foreign state.

(d) The President shall, from time to time by proclamation, definitely enumerate the arms, ammunition, and implements of war, the export of which is prohibited by this section. . . .

(e) Whoever, in violation of any of the provisions of this Act, shall export, or attempt to export, or cause to be exported, arms, ammunition, or implements of war from the United States shall be fined not more than $10,000, or imprisoned not more than five years, or both. . . .

Section 3. (a) Whenever the President shall have issued a proclamation under the authority of section 1 of this Act, it shall thereafter be unlawful for any person within the United States to purchase, sell, or exchange bonds, securities, or other obligations of the government of any belligerent state or of any state wherein civil strife exists, named in such proclamation, . . . or to make any loan or extend any credit to any such government. . . .

(b) The provisions of this section shall not apply to a renewal or adjustment of such indebtedness as may exist on the date of the President's proclamation.

(c) Whoever shall violate the provisions of this section or of any regulations issued hereunder shall, upon conviction thereof, be fined not more than $50,000 or imprisoned for not more than five years, or both. Should the violation be by a corporation, organization, or association, each officer or agent thereof participating in the violation may be liable to the penalty herein prescribed. . . .

Section 4. This Act shall not apply to an American republic or republics engaged in war against a non-American state or states, provided the American republic is not cooperating with a non-American state or states in such war.

Section 5. (a) There is hereby established a National Munitions Control Board (hereinafter referred to as the "Board") to carry out the provisions of this Act. . . .

Section 6. (a) Whenever the President shall have issued a proclamation under the authority of section 1 of this Act, it shall thereafter be unlawful, until such proclamation is revoked, for any American vessel to carry any arms, ammunition, or implements of war to any belligerent state, or to any state where civil strife exists, named in such proclamation, or to any neutral state for transshipment. . . .

Section 9. Whenever the President shall have issued a proclamation under the authority of section 1 of this Act it shall thereafter be unlawful for any citizen of the United States to travel on any vessel of the state or states named in such proclamation, except in accordance with such rules and regulations as the President shall prescribe. . . .

Section 10. Whenever the President shall have issued a proclamation under the authority of section 1, it shall thereafter be unlawful, until such proclamation is revoked, for any American vessel engaged in commerce with any belligerent state, or any state wherein civil strife exists, named in such proclamation, to be armed or to carry any armament, arms, ammunition, or implements of war, except small arms and ammunition therefor which the President may deem necessary and shall publicly designate for the preservation of discipline aboard such vessels. . . .

— 49 —

ROOSEVELT'S QUARANTINE SPEECH, OCTOBER 5, 1937 [1]

President Roosevelt had doubts about the Neutrality Act he signed in May, 1937, since its application might aid an aggressor or penalize a victim of aggression. When Japan began full-scale war against China in July, the President decided not to invoke the act on the ground that there had been no declaration of war and in October he delivered his famous Quarantine speech in Chicago which stressed the need of collective measures to halt aggression. The phrases which caused a violent public reaction Mr. Roosevelt himself had inserted in an inoffensive speech the State Department had prepared for him. Mr. Hull was shocked and later wrote that the incident had set back "our constant educational campaign" for international cooperation by six months. At his press conference the next day the President said nothing to alarm the isolationists, and his public pronouncements thereafter, right up to Pearl Harbor, minimized the possibility of American involvement abroad.

⚹   ⚹   ⚹

. . . Some fifteen years ago the hopes of mankind for a continuing era of international peace were raised to great heights when more than sixty nations solemnly

[1] From Samuel I. Rosenman, ed., *The Public Papers and Addresses of Franklin D. Roosevelt* (New York, 1941), 1937 vol., pp. 406-411.

pledged themselves not to resort to arms in furtherance of their national aims and policies. The high aspirations expressed in the Briand-Kellogg Peace Pact and the hopes for peace thus raised have of late given way to a haunting fear of calamity. The present reign of terror and international lawlessness began a few years ago.

It began through unjustified interference in the internal affairs of other nations or the invasion of alien territory in violation of treaties; and has now reached a stage where the very foundations of civilization are seriously threatened. . . .

How happy we are that the circumstances of the moment permit us to put our money into bridges and boulevards, dams and reforestation, the conservation of our soil and many other kinds of useful works rather than into huge standing armies and vast supplies of implements of war.

I am compelled and you are compelled, nevertheless, to look ahead. The peace, the freedom and the security of ninety percent of the population of the world is being jeopardized by the remaining ten percent who are threatening a breakdown of all international order and law. Surely the ninety percent who want to live in peace under law and in accordance with moral standards that have received almost universal acceptance through the centuries, can and must find some way to make their will prevail. . . .

It seems to be unfortunately true that the epidemic of world lawlessness is spreading.

When an epidemic of physical disease starts to spread, the community approves and joins in a quarantine of the patients in order to protect the health of the community against the spread of the disease. . . .

War is a contagion, whether it be declared or undeclared. It can engulf states and peoples remote from the original scene of the hostilities. We are determined to keep out of war, yet we cannot insure ourselves against the disastrous effects of war and the dangers of involvement. We are adopting such measures as will minimize our risk of involvement, but we cannot have complete protection in a world of disorder in which confidence and security have broken down.

If civilization is to survive the principles of the Prince

of Peace must be restored. Trust between nations must be revived.

Most important of all, the will for peace on the part of peace-loving nations must express itself to the end that nations that may be tempted to violate their agreements and the rights of others will desist from such a course. There must be positive endeavors to preserve peace.

America hates war. America hopes for peace. Therefore, America actively engages in the search for peace.

— 50 —

ROOSEVELT'S REQUEST FOR REPEAL OF THE ARMS EMBARGO, SEPTEMBER 21, 1939[1]

When World War II began, President Roosevelt issued the traditional proclamation of neutrality, and also invoked the Neutrality Act whose embargo on the export of arms and ammunition he had recently branded an encouragement to aggressors. He then called a special session of Congress and asked for revision of the Neutrality Act to permit the sale and export of arms and munitions to belligerents on a "cash-and-carry" basis. His message to Congress makes no mention of the desirability of aiding the opponents of Hitler, which he had in mind, but emphasized the remaining provisions of the Neutrality Act which would keep the United States out of the war. The repeal was voted by the Senate 63-30 on October 27, by the House 243-181 on November 2.

✓   ✓   ✓

[1] Rosenman, ed., *The Public Papers and Addresses of Franklin D. Roosevelt,* 1939 vol., pp. 512-522.

I have asked Congress to reassemble in extraordinary session in order that it may consider and act on the amendment of certain legislation, which, in my best judgment, so alters the historic foreign policy of the United States that it impairs the peaceful relations of the United States with foreign nations. . . .

Beginning with the foundation of our constitutional Government in the year 1789, the American policy in respect to belligerent nations, with one notable exception, has been based on international law. . . .

The single exception to which I refer was the policy adopted by this nation during the Napoleonic Wars, when, seeking to avoid involvement, we acted for some years under the so-called Embargo and Non-Intercourse Acts. That policy turned out to be a disastrous failure. . . .

Our next deviation by statute from the sound principles of neutrality and peace through international law did not come for one hundred and thirty years. It was the so-called Neutrality Act of 1935—only four years ago—an Act continued in force by the Joint Resolution of May 1, 1937, despite grave doubts expressed as to its wisdom by many Senators and Representatives and by officials charged with the conduct of our foreign relations, including myself.

I regret that the Congress passed that Act. I regret equally that I signed that Act.

On July fourteenth of this year, I asked the Congress in the cause of peace and in the interest of real American neutrality and security, to take action to change that Act.

I now ask again that such action be taken in respect to that part of the Act which is wholly inconsistent with ancient precepts of the law of nations—the embargo provisions. I ask it because they are, in my opinion, most vitally dangerous to American neutrality, American security and, above all, American peace. . . .

It has been erroneously said that return to that policy might bring us nearer to war. I give to you my deep and unalterable conviction, based on years of experience as a worker in the field of international peace, that by the repeal of the embargo the United States will more probably remain at peace than if the law remains as it stands today. I say this because with the repeal of the embargo, this Government clearly and definitely will insist that American citizens and American ships keep away from the immediate perils of the actual zones of conflict.

Repeal of the embargo and a return to international law are the crux of the issue that faces us.

The enactment of the embargo provisions did more than merely reverse our traditional policy. It had the effect of putting land powers on the same footing as naval powers, so far as seaborne commerce was concerned. A land power which threatened war could thus feel assured in advance that any prospective sea-power antagonist would be weakened through denial of its ancient right to buy anything anywhere. This, four years ago, began to give a definite advantage to one belligerent as against another, not through his own strength or geographical position, but through an affirmative act on the part of the United States. Removal of the embargo is merely reverting to the sounder international practice, and pursuing in time of war as in time of peace our ordinary trade policies. . . .

I believe that American merchant vessels should, as far as possible, be restricted from entering war zones. . . .

The second objective is to prevent American citizens from traveling on belligerent vessels, or in danger areas. . . .

The third objective, requiring the foreign buyer to take transfer of title in this country to commodities purchased by belligerents, is also a result that can be attained by legislation or substantially achieved through due notice by proclamation.

The fourth objective is the preventing of war credits to belligerents. . . .

The result of these last two objectives will be to require all purchases to be made in cash, and all cargoes to be carried in the purchasers' own ships, at the purchasers' own risk. . . .

To those who say that this program would involve a step toward war on our part, I reply that it offers far greater safeguards than we now possess or have ever possessed, to protect American lives and property from danger. It is a positive program for giving safety. This means less likelihood of incidents and controversies which tend to draw us into conflict, as they unhappily did in the last World War. There lies the road to peace! . . .

— 51 —

CANADIAN-AMERICAN DEFENSE, AUGUST 18, 1940[1]

Shortly after the fall of France and during the Battle of Britain President Roosevelt and Prime Minister Mac-Kenzie King of Canada met at Ogdensburg, New York, to discuss common problems of North American defense. The statement that was issued at the end of their talks was laconic, but made it clear that Canadian-American resources would be pooled and efforts joined in defending one-fourth of the globe. The work of the Joint Board then agreed upon developed a pattern of collaboration for security which continued into the postwar era.

The Prime Minister and the President have discussed the mutual problems of defense in relation to the safety of Canada and the United States.

It has been agreed that a Permanent Joint Board on Defense shall be set up at once by the two countries.

This permanent Joint Board on Defense shall commence immediate studies relating to sea, land and air problems including personnel and materiel.

It will consider in the broad sense the defense of the north half of the Western Hemisphere.

The Permanent Joint Board on Defense will consist of four or five members from each country, most of them from the services. It will meet shortly.

[1] From *Department of State Bulletin*, III, No. 61 (Aug. 24, 1940), p. 154.

DESTROYERS FOR BASES, SEPTEMBER 2, 1940[1]

The sudden collapse of France in the summer of 1940 greatly increased American concern over the war in Europe. As master of the continent, Hitler could expand his empire to the New World if Britain fell and Germany took over the British and French navies. The Roosevelt administration intensified efforts to arm, induced Congress to pass the first peace-time conscription act, and strengthened Great Britain's power of resistance by the celebrated swap of bases for destroyers. In exchange for Atlantic bases leased for 99 years, the United States gave Britain 50 destroyers of World War I vintage which served to protect convoys against German submarines. President Roosevelt carried out the exchange by executive agreement, and then informed Congress.

✓   ✓   ✓

MESSAGE TO THE CONGRESS

I transmit herewith for the information of the Congress notes exchanged between the British Ambassador at Washington and the Secretary of State on September 2, 1940, under which this Government has acquired the right to lease naval and air bases in Newfoundland, and in the islands of Bermuda, the Bahamas, Jamaica, St. Lucia, Trinidad, and Antigua, and in British Guiana; also a copy of an opinion by the Attorney General dated August 27, 1940, regarding my authority to consummate this arrangement.

The right to bases in Newfoundland and Bermuda are gifts—generously given and gladly received. The other

[1] *Department of State Bulletin,* 3, No. 63 (Sept. 7, 1940), p. 201.

bases mentioned have been acquired in exchange for fifty of our over-age destroyers.

This is not inconsistent in any sense with our status of peace. Still less is it a threat against any nation. It is an epochal and far-reaching act of preparation for continental defense in the face of grave danger.

Preparation for defense is an inalienable prerogative of a sovereign state. Under present circumstances this exercise of sovereign right is essential to the maintenance of our peace and safety. This is the most important action in the reinforcement of our national defense that has been taken since the Louisiana Purchase. Then as now, considerations of safety from overseas attack were fundamental. The value to the Western Hemisphere of these outposts of security is beyond calculation. Their need has long been recognized by our country, and especially by those primarily charged with the duty of charting and organizing our own naval and military defense. They are essential to the protection of the Panama Canal, Central America, the Northern portion of South America, the Antilles, Canada, Mexico, and our own Eastern and Gulf Seaboards. Their consequent importance in hemispheric defense is obvious. For these reasons I have taken advantage of the present opportunity to acquire them.

FRANKLIN D. ROOSEVELT

— 53 —

LEND-LEASE ACT, MARCH 11, 1941[1]

Repeal of the arms embargo in 1939 enabled Britain and France to obtain arms in the United States if paid

[1] From *United States Statutes at Large*, 55, Pt. 1, pp. 31-33.

*for and carried in their own ships. By the end of 1940
France had been defeated and British funds were running
out. The United States was still technically neutral, but
the Roosevent administration was determined to do everything short of war to keep Britain fighting. However, the
President was strongly opposed to government loans which
would complicate and embitter postwar relations. He
finally solved the problem of financing the enemies of Germany without hangover by a simple analogy: "Suppose
your neighbor's house catches fire, you would immediately lend him your garden hose, if only out of self-inter-
est." By lending and leasing war materials, instead of
selling them, the United States kept the dollar sign out of
its transactions with nations whose defense was deemed
"vital to the defense of the United States." By V-J day
goods and services valued at more than $50 billion had
gone out under Lend-Lease to help defeat the Axis
powers.*

✓   ✓   ✓

Section 3. (a) Notwithstanding the provisions of any
other law, the President may, from time to time, when he
deems it in the interest of national defense, authorize the
Secretary of War, the Secretary of the Navy, or the head
of any other department or agency of the Government—

(1) To manufacture in arsenals, factories, and shipyards under their jurisdiction, or otherwise procure, to
the extent to which funds are made available therefor, or
contracts are authorized from time to time by the Congress, or both, any defense article for the government of
any country whose defense the President deems vital to
the defense of the United States.

(2) To sell, transfer title to, exchange, lease, lend, or
otherwise dispose of, to any such government any defense
article, but no defense article not manufactured or procured under paragraph (1) shall be in any way disposed
of under this paragraph, except after consultation with
the Chief of Staff of the Army or the Chief of Naval
Operations of the Navy or, both. . . .

(3) To test, inspect, prove, repair, outfit, recondition,
or otherwise to place in good working order, to the extent to which funds are made available therefor, or
contracts are authorized from time to time by the Con-

gress, or both, any defense article for any such government, or to procure any or all such services by private contract. . . .

(b) The terms and conditions upon which any such foreign government receives any aid authorized under subsection (a) shall be those which the President deems satisfactory, and the benefit to the United States may be payment or repayment in kind or property, or any other direct or indirect benefit which the President deems satisfactory. . . .

(d) Nothing in this Act shall be construed to authorize or to permit the authorization of convoying vessels by naval vessels of the United States.

(e) Nothing in this Act shall be construed to authorize or to permit the authorization of the entry of any American vessel into a combat area in violation of section 3 of the Neutrality Act of 1939. . . .

— 54 —

THE ATLANTIC CHARTER
AUGUST 14, 1941 [1]

The Lend-Lease Act was a material milestone on the road to belligerency; the Atlantic Charter definitely aligned the United States with Great Britain in a joint statement of war aims comparable to Wilson's Fourteen Points. The Charter was drawn up in August 1941 when Roosevelt and Churchill and their staffs met for a shipboard conference off Argentia, Newfoundland. In his message to Congress the preceding January, the President had stated as high objectives for mankind freedom of speech, freedom of religion, freedom from want, and

[1] From *Peace and War,* Department of State Publication 1983, pp. 718-719.

freedom from fear. The Atlantic Charter was built on a draft by the Prime Minister who had forgotten two of Roosevelt's four freedoms, and no one reminded him. However, Roosevelt insisted on deleting Churchill's reference to "effective international organization," and the eighth point touches only lightly on the thought of an eventual "system of general security."

✓   ✓   ✓

Joint declaration of the President of the United States of America and the Prime Minister, Mr. Churchill, representing His Majesty's Government in the United Kingdom, being met together, deem it right to make known certain common principles in the national policies of their respective countries on which they base their hopes for a better future for the world.

First, their countries seek no aggrandizement, territorial or other;

Second, they desire to see no territorial changes that do not accord with the freely expressed wishes of the peoples concerned;

Third, they respect the right of all peoples to choose the form of government under which they will live; and they wish to see sovereign rights and self-government restored to those who have been forcibly deprived of them;

Fourth, they will endeavor, with due respect for their existing obligations, to further the enjoyment by all states, great or small, victor or vanquished, of access, on equal terms, to the trade and to the raw materials of the world which are needed for their economic prosperity;

Fifth, they desire to bring about the fullest collaboration between all nations in the economic field with the object of securing, for all, improved labor standards, economic advancement, and social security;

Sixth, after the final destruction of the Nazi tyranny, they hope to see established a peace which will afford to all nations the means of dwelling in safety within their own boundaries, and which will afford assurance that all the men in all the lands may live out their lives in freedom from fear and want;

Seventh, such a peace should enable all men to traverse the high seas and oceans without hindrance;

Eighth, they believe that all the nations of the world, for realistic as well as spiritual reasons, must come to the abandonment of the use of force. Since no future peace can be maintained if land, sea, or air armaments continue to be employed by nations which threaten, or may threaten, aggression outside of their frontiers, they believe, pending the establishment of a wider and permanent system of general security, that the disarmament of such nations is essential. They will likewise aid and encourage all other practicable measures which will lighten for peace-loving peoples the crushing burden of armaments.

FRANKLIN D. ROOSEVELT
WINSTON S. CHURCHILL

— 55 —

FINAL AMERICAN TERMS TO JAPAN, NOVEMBER 26, 1941[1]

While the United States was drawn toward belligerency by German victories in Europe, Germany's ally, Japan, planned to expand its "new order" southward to include the colonies of occupied France and the Netherlands. To lessen the risk of complications, Japan concluded a pact of neutrality with Russia in April, 1941; and for eight months before Pearl Harbor sought an accord with Washington which had clearly indicated its disapproval of Japanese empire-building. On September 6, 1941, the Japanese government decided on war with the United States if diplomacy failed; and on November 20 Japan's

[1] From *Peace and War,* Department of State Publication 1983, pp. 810-812.

final terms for an accord were given Secretary Hull by Ambassadors Nomura and Kurusu. These terms left Japan dominant in China and capable of southward expansion, and they were rejected by the United States government. On November 26 Secretary Hull presented the terms of an accord that would be acceptable to the United States. Since Mr. Hull knew from intercepted radio messages that our rejection of the final Japanese proposals was to be followed by war, his note of November 26 in effect states what the United States would fight for in the Pacific. Actually by that date the Japanese task force had started on its fateful mission to the Hawaiian Islands.

✓   ✓   ✓

SECTION I   Draft Mutual Declaration of Policy

The Government of the United States and the Government of Japan both being solicitous for the peace of the Pacific affirm that their national policies are directed toward lasting and extensive peace throughout the Pacific area, that they have no territorial designs in that area, that they have no intention of threatening other countries or of using military force aggressively against any neighboring nation. . . .

SECTION II   Steps to be taken by the Government of the United States and by the Government of Japan

1. The Government of the United States and the Government of Japan will endeavor to conclude a multilateral non-aggression pact among the British Empire, China, Japan, the Netherlands, the Soviet Union, Thailand and the United States.

2. Both Governments will endeavor to conclude among the American, British, Chinese, Japanese, the Netherland and Thai Governments an agreement whereunder each of the Governments would pledge itself to respect the territorial integrity of French Indochina. . . .

3. The Government of Japan will withdraw all military, naval, air and police forces from China and from Indochina.

4. The Government of the United States and the Government of Japan will not support—militarily, politically, economically—any government or regime in China

other than the National Government of the Republic of China with capital temporarily at Chungking.

5. Both Governments will give up all extraterritorial rights in China, including rights and interests in and with regard to international settlements and concessions, and rights under the Boxer Protocol of 1901. . . .

6. The Government of the United States and the Government of Japan will enter into negotiations for the conclusion between the United States and Japan of a trade agreement, based upon reciprocal most-favored-nation treatment and reduction of trade barriers by both countries, including an undertaking by the United States to bind raw silk on the free list.

7. The Government of the United States and the Government of Japan will, respectively, remove the freezing restrictions on Japanese funds in the United States and on American funds in Japan.

8. Both Governments will agree upon a plan for the stabilization of the dollar-yen rate, with the allocation of funds adequate for this purpose, half to be supplied by Japan and half by the United States.

9. Both Governments will agree that no agreement which either has concluded with any third power or powers shall be interpreted by it in such a way as to conflict with the fundamental purpose of this agreement, the establishment and preservation of peace throughout the Pacific area.

10. Both Governments will use their influence to cause other governments to adhere to and to give practical application to the basic political and economic principles set forth in this agreement.

ROOSEVELT'S WAR MESSAGE TO THE NATION, DECEMBER 9, 1941[1]

The Japanese attack on Pearl Harbor dramatically terminated the debate on peace or war in Congress and in the nation. On the following day President Roosevelt delivered his war message to Congress, and the war resolution was passed unanimously in the Senate and 388 to 1 in the House. In addressing Congress the President had mentioned no enemy but Japan, but a day later in his radio address to the nation he developed the theme that Japan, Italy, and Germany were partners and that the grand strategy of the United States and its allies must be based on that assumption. Whatever doubts anyone had about that assumption expired on December 11 when Germany and Italy declared war on the United States.

✓　　　　✓　　　　✓

The sudden criminal attacks perpetrated by the Japanese in the Pacific provide the climax of a decade of international immorality.

Powerful and resourceful gangsters have banded together to make war upon the whole human race. Their challenge has now been flung at the United States of America. The Japanese have treacherously violated the long-standing peace between us. Many American soldiers and sailors have been killed by enemy action. American ships have been sunk; American airplanes have been destroyed.

The Congress and the people of the United States have accepted that challenge.

[1] From *Peace and War,* Department of State Publication 1983, pp. 842-848.

Together with other free peoples, we are now fighting to maintain our right to live among our world neighbors in freedom and in common decency, without fear of assault. . . .

The course that Japan has followed for the past 10 years in Asia has paralleled the course of Hitler and Mussolini in Europe and Africa. Today, it has become far more than a parallel. It is collaboration so well calculated that all the continents of the world, and all the oceans, are now considered by the Axis strategists as one gigantic battlefield. . . .

In these past few years—and, most violently, in the past few days—we have learned a terrible lesson. It is our obligation to our dead—it is our sacred obligation to their children and our children—that we must never forget what we have learned. And what we all have learned is this:

There is no such thing as security for any nation—or any individual—in a world ruled by the principles of gangsterism. There is no such thing as impregnable defense against powerful aggressors who sneak up in the dark and strike without warning. We have learned that our ocean-girt hemisphere is not immune from severe attack—that we cannot measure our safety in terms of miles on any map. . . .

Your Government knows that for weeks Germany has been telling Japan that if Japan did not attack the United States, Japan would not share in dividing the spoils with Germany when peace came. . . .

We also know that Germany and Japan are conducting their military and naval operations in accordance with a joint plan. That plan considers all peoples and nations which are not helping the Axis powers as common enemies of each and every one of the Axis powers.

That is their simple and obvious grand strategy. That is why the American people must realize that it can be matched only with similar grand strategy. We must realize for example that Japanese successes against the United States in the Pacific are helpful to German operations in Libya; that any German success against the Caucasus is inevitably an assistance to Japan in her operations against the Dutch East Indies; that a German attack against Algiers or Morocco opens the way to a German attack against South America. . . .

Remember always that Germany and Italy, regardless of any formal declaration of war, consider themselves at war with the United States at this moment just as much as they consider themselves at war with Britain and Russia. And Germany puts all the other republics of the Americas into the category of enemies. The people of the hemisphere can be honored by that. . . .

We are now in the midst of a war, not for conquest, not for vengeance, but for a world in which this Nation, and all that this Nation represents, will be safe for our children. We expect to eliminate the danger from Japan, but it would serve us ill if we accomplished that and found that the rest of the world was dominated by Hitler and Mussolini.

We are going to win the war and we are going to win the peace that follows.

And in the dark hours of this day—and through dark days that may be yet to come—we will know that the vast majority of the members of the human race are on our side. Many of them are fighting with us. All of them are praying for us. For, in representing our cause, we represent theirs as well—our hope and their hope for liberty under God.

— 57 —

DECLARATION BY THE UNITED NATIONS, JANUARY 1, 1942[1]

Soon after Pearl Harbor, Prime Minister Churchill came to the United States for conferences on war plans.

[1] From *Peace and War*, Department of State Publication 1983, pp. 850-853.

He and President Roosevelt turned first to the formation of a coalition of all enemies of the Axis powers. This was achieved by means of a collective executive agreement drafted by Churchill and Roosevelt and signed by twenty-six nations and published on January 1 as a Declaration of the United Nations. "This prelude to a new world symphony," Robert Sherwood remarked, was being composed "against the reverberations of shocking defeats in the Pacific."

✐   ✐   ✐

A Joint Declaration by the United States, the United Kingdom, the Union of Soviet Socialist Republics, China, Australia, Belgium, Canada, Costa Rica, Cuba, Czechoslovakia, Dominican Republic, El Salvador, Greece, Guatemala, Haiti, Honduras, India, Luxembourg, Netherlands, New Zealand, Nicaragua, Norway, Panama, Poland, South Africa, Yugoslavia.

The Governments signatory hereto,

Having subscribed to a common program of purposes and principles embodied in the Joint Declaration of the President of the United States and the Prime Minister of the United Kingdom of Great Britain and Northern Ireland dated August 14, 1941, known as the Atlantic Charter,

Being convinced that complete victory over their enemies is essential to defend life, liberty, independence and religious freedom and to preserve human rights and justice in their own lands as well as in other lands, and that they are now engaged in a common struggle against savage and brutal forces seeking to subjugate the world,

DECLARE:

(1) Each Government pledges itself to employ its full resources, military or economic, against those members of the Tripartite Pact and its adherents with which such government is at war.

(2) Each Government pledges itself to cooperate with the Governments signatory hereto and not to make a separate armistice or peace with the enemies.

The foregoing declaration may be adhered to by other nations which are, or which may be, rendering material assistance and contributions in the struggle for victory over Hitlerism.

RENUNCIATION OF EXTRATERRITORIAL RIGHTS IN CHINA, JANUARY 11, 1943[1]

As a non-belligerent the United States had helped China to defend itself against Japan with loans and Lend-Lease supplies, and after Pearl Harbor Washington valued China both as a co-belligerent and as a potential stabilizing force in postwar Asia. But the Allied strategy of defeating Germany before Japan, and what General Marshall termed "unparallelled logistical problems" convinced Chiang Kai-shek's government that China was not getting its fair share of airplanes and guns. The State Department attempted to compensate China for material neglect by abrogating the "unequal treaties" and persuaded Great Britain to do the same. Concurrently, Congress repealed the Chinese Exclusion Act and gave Chinese nationals a regular immigration quota and the right of naturalization. This agreement was made in Washington and signed by Secretary Hull and Wei Tao-Ming, the Chinese Ambassador.

✓ ✓ ✓

ARTICLE I. All those provisions of treaties or agreements in force between the United States of America and the Republic of China which authorize the Government of the United States or its representatives to exercise jurisdiction over nationals of the United States in the

---

[1] From *United States Relations with China,* Department of State Publication 3573, Far Eastern Series 30, 1949, pp. 514-517.

territory of the Republic of China are hereby abrogated. Nationals of the United States in such territory shall be subject to the jurisdiction of the Government of the Republic of China in accordance with the principles of international law and practice.

ARTICLE II. The Government of the United States considers that the Final Protocol concluded at Peking on September 7, 1901, between the Chinese Government and other governments, including the Government of the United States, should be terminated and agrees that the rights accorded to the Government of the United States under that Protocol and under agreements supplementary thereto shall cease. . . .

ARTICLE III. The Government of the United States considers that the International Settlements at Shanghai and Amoy should revert to the administration and control of the Government of the Republic of China and agrees that the rights accorded to the Government of the United States in relation to those settlements shall cease. . . .

— 59 —

THE CONNALLY RESOLUTION, NOVEMBER 5, 1943[1]

During the first half of World War II, the Roosevelt administration carried on as inconspicuously as possible a limited amount of postwar planning while postponing as politically inexpedient any commitment to a new structure comparable to the League of Nations. However, during 1943, opinion polls and resolutions in both Houses of Congress revealed increasing support for an effective

[1] From Senate Committee on Foreign Relations, *A Decade of American Foreign Policy*, p. 14.

*international organization, and in October of that year
the United States government for the first time pledged
itself to the idea of a new world organization in a Four
Power declaration at Moscow. The most convincing
evidence that such an organization would not meet the
fate of the League in the Senate was the vote of 85 to 5
for the resolution of Senator Tom Connally of Texas,
chairman of the Senate Foreign Relations Committee,
which is reprinted here.*

↑   ↑   ↑

Resolved, That the war against all our enemies be
waged until complete victory is achieved.

That the United States cooperate with its comrades-in-
arms in securing a just and honorable peace.

That the United States, acting through its constitutional
processes, join with free and sovereign nations in the
establishment and maintenance of international authority
with power to prevent aggression and to preserve the
peace of the world.

That the Senate recognizes the necessity of there being
established at the earliest practicable date a general international organization, based on the principle of the
sovereign equality of all peace-loving states, and open to
membership by all such states, large and small, for the
maintenance of international peace and security.

That, pursuant to the Constitution of the United States,
any treaty made to effect the purpose of this resolution,
on behalf of the Government of the United States with
any other nation or any associations of nations, shall be
made only by and with the advice and consent of the
Senate of the United States, provided two-thirds of the
Senators present concur.

YALTA AGREEMENTS,
FEBRUARY 11, 1945[1]

With the Germans on the run, Roosevelt and Churchill joined Stalin at Yalta on the Crimean peninsula on February 4, 1945, and with their staffs the Big Three discussed a wide range of basic questions relating to the war and the peace. The German problem, including the amount of reparations, was left to later decision. Agreement was reached on the principle of self-determination for the liberated states of Eastern Europe, although their choices were certain to be narrowed by the presence of Russian troops. Unresolved questions about the United Nations, including the veto, were settled to everyone's satisfaction. Finally, the Soviet Union was paid the price it demanded for entering the war against Japan when Germany was dealt with. This has been the most controversial and is perhaps the least defensible of the decisions made at Yalta. It was kept secret until February, 1946.

✓　　　　✓　　　　✓

The Crimea Conference of the Heads of the Governments of the United States, the United Kingdom, and the Union of Soviet Socialist Republics which took place from February 4th to 11th came to the following conclusions.

I. World Organization. It was decided:

(1) that a United Nations Conference on the proposed world organization should be summoned for Wednesday, 25th April, 1945, and should be held in the United States of America.

(2) the Nations to be invited to this Conference should be: (a) the United Nations as they existed on the 8th

[1] From *Foreign Relations of the United States, the Conferences at Malta and Yalta, 1945* (Washington, 1955), pp. 975-984.

February, 1945 and (b) such of the Associated Nations as have declared war on the common enemy by 1st March, 1945. . . . When the Conference on World Organization is held, the delegates of the United Kingdom and United States will support a proposal to admit to original membership two Soviet Socialist Republics, i.e. the Ukraine and White Russia.

(3) that the United States Government on behalf of the Three Powers should consult the Government of China and the French Provisional Government in regard to the decisions taken at the present Conference concerning the proposed World Organization.

(4) . . . The above-named governments suggest that the Conference consider as affording a basis for such a Charter the Proposals for the Establishment of a General International Organization, which were made public last October as a result of the Dumbarton Oaks Conference, and which have now been supplemented by the following provisions for Section C of Chapter VI:

C. Voting

1. Each member of the Security Council should have one vote.

2. Decisions of the Security Council on procedural matters should be made by an affirmative vote of seven members.

3. Decisions of the Security Council on all other matters should be made by an affirmative vote of seven members including the concurring votes of the permanent members; provided that, in decisions under Chapter VIII, Section A (Pacific Settlement of Disputes) and under the second sentence of paragraph 1 of Chapter VIII, Section C (Encouragement of the Settlement of Disputes through Regional Agencies), a party to a dispute should abstain from voting. . . .

II. Declaration on Liberated Europe. The Premier of the Union of Soviet Socialist Republics, the Prime Minister of the United Kingdom and the President of the United States . . . jointly declare their mutual agreement to concert during the temporary period of instability in liberated Europe the policies of their three governments in assisting the peoples liberated from the domination of Nazi Germany and the peoples of the former Axis satellite states of Europe to solve by democratic means their pressing political and economic problems. . . .

III. Dismemberment of Germany

. . . . The study of the procedure for the dismemberment of Germany was referred to a Committee consisting of Mr. Eden, Mr. Winant and Mr. Gousev. . . .

VII. Poland. A new situation has been created in Poland as a result of her complete liberation by the Red Army. This calls for the establishment of a Polish Provisional Government which can be more broadly based than was possible before the recent liberation of the Western part of Poland. The Provisional Government which is now functioning in Poland should therefore be reorganized on a broader democratic basis with the inclusion of democratic leaders from Poland itself and from Poles abroad. This new Government should then be called the Polish Provisional Government of National Unity. . . .

The three Heads of Government consider that the Eastern frontier of Poland should follow the Curzon Line with digressions from it in some regions of five to eight kilometres in favour of Poland. They recognize that Poland must receive substantial accessions of territory in the North and West. They feel that the opinion of the new Polish Provisional Government of National Unity should be sought in due course on the extent of these accessions and that the final delimitation of the Western frontier of Poland should thereafter await the Peace Conference. . . .

E. R. Stettinius, Jr.
V. Molotov
Anthony Eden

Agreement Regarding Entry of the Soviet Union into the War Against Japan

The leaders of the three Great Powers—the Soviet Union, the United States and Great Britain—have agreed that in two or three months after Germany has surrendered and the war in Europe has terminated the Soviet Union shall enter into the war against Japan on the side of the Allies on condition that:

1. The status quo in Outer-Mongolia (The Mongolian People's Republic) shall be preserved;

2. The former rights of Russia violated by the treacherous attack of Japan in 1904 shall be restored, viz.:

(a) the southern part of Sakhalin as well as all the islands adjacent to it shall be returned to the Soviet Union,

(b) the commercial port of Dairen shall be internationalized, the preeminent interests of the Soviet Union in this port being safeguarded and the lease of Port Arthur as a naval base of the U.S.S.R. restored,

(c) the Chinese-Eastern Railroad and the South-Manchurian Railroad which provides an outlet to Dairen shall be jointly operated by the establishment of a joint Soviet-Chinese Company it being understood that the preeminent interests of the Soviet Union shall be safeguarded and that China shall retain full sovereignty in Manchuria;

3. The Kuril islands shall be handed over to the Soviet Union.

It is understood, that the agreement concerning Outer-Mongolia and the ports and railroads referred to above will require the concurrence of Generalissimo Chiang Kai-shek. The President will take measures in order to obtain this concurrence on advice from Marshal Stalin.

The heads of the three Great Powers have agreed that these claims of the Soviet Union shall be unquestionably fulfilled after Japan has been defeated.

For its part the Soviet Union expresses its readiness to conclude with the National Government of China a pact of friendship and alliance between the U.S.S.R. and China in order to render assistance to China with its armed forces for the purpose of liberating China from the Japanese yoke.

J. STALIN
FRANKLIN D. ROOSEVELT
WINSTON S. CHURCHILL

— 61 —

ACT OF CHAPULTEPEC, MARCH 8, 1945[1]

The Inter-American Conference which met in Mexico City toward the end of World War II devoted much of its attention to procedures and institutions that would strengthen the "Inter-American System," and provide security on a regional basis. The Act of Chapultepec, reprinted below, established a temporary structure for dealing with aggression. At San Francisco the United Nations gave its sanction to the Act by recognizing the "inherent right" of collective self-defense in Article 51. A permanent regional system for the American states was agreed upon at Rio de Janeiro in 1947, and served as a model for the North American Treaty Organization.

✦   ✦   ✦

Part I

The Governments Represented at the Inter-American Conference on Problems of War and Peace *Declare*:

1. That all sovereign States are juridically equal among themselves.

2. That every State has the right to the respect of its individuality and independence, on the part of the other members of the international community.

3. That every attack of a State against the integrity or the inviolability of the territory or against the sovereignty or political independence of an American State, shall, comformably to Part III hereof, be considered as an act of aggression against the other States which sign this Act. . . .

[1] From Manley O. Hudson, ed., *International Legislation, a Collection of Texts of Multipartite International Instruments* (New York, 1950), IX, pp. 284-289.

Part II

The Inter-American Conference on Problems of War and Peace *Recommends*:

That for the purpose of meeting threats or acts of aggression against any American Republic following the establishment of peace, the Governments of the American Republics consider the conclusion, in accordance with their constitutional processes, of a treaty establishing procedures whereby such threats or acts may be met by the use, by all or some of the signatories of said treaty, of any one or more of the following measures; recall of chiefs of diplomatic missions; breaking of diplomatic relations, breaking of consular relations; breaking of postal, telegraphic, telephonic, radio-telephonic relations; interruption of economic, commercial and financial relations; use of armed force to prevent or repel aggression.

Part III

The above Declaration and Recommendation constitute a regional arrangement for dealing with such matters relating to the maintenance of international peace and security as are appropriate for regional action in this Hemisphere. The said arrangement, and the pertinent activities and procedures, shall be consistent with the purposes and principles of the general international organization, when established. This agreement shall be known as the "ACT OF CHAPULTEPEC."

— 62 —

THE POTSDAM CONFERENCE, JULY 17-AUGUST 2, 1945 [1]

At the final summit meeting of the three wartime Allies, the veteran Stalin faced two new heads of govern-

[1] From Senate Committee on Foreign Relations, *A Decade of American Foreign Policy*, pp. 34-48.

ment. Harry S. Truman had become President at the death of Roosevelt in April, and halfway through the conference Clement Attlee took Churchill's seat when British elections were won by the Labour party. Big Three unity was still evident in the agreement on machinery and principles for dealing with Germany, but it was obvious that success in carrying out the agreement must depend on a solidarity that was not likely to survive long into the postwar era.

The Principles to Govern the Treatment of Germany in the Initial Control Period.

A. POLITICAL PRINCIPLES

1. In accordance with the Agreement on Control Machinery in Germany, supreme authority in Germany is exercised, on instructions from their respective Governments, by the Commanders-in-Chief of the armed forces of the United States, the United Kingdom, the Union of Soviet Socialist Republics, and the French Republic, each in his own zone of occupation, and also jointly, in matters affecting Germany as a whole, in their capacity as members of the Control Council.

2. So far as is practicable, there shall be uniformity of treatment of the German population throughout Germany.

3. The purposes of the occupation of Germany by which the Control Council shall be guided are:

(i) The complete disarmament and demilitarization of Germany and the elimination or control of all German industry that could be used for military production. . . .

(ii) To convince the German people that they have suffered a total military defeat and that they cannot escape responsibility for what they have brought upon themselves . . .

(iii) To destroy the National Socialist Party and its affiliated and supervised organizations, to dissolve all Nazi institutions . . .

(iv) To prepare for the eventual reconstruction of German political life on a democratic basis and for eventual peaceful cooperation in international life by Germany.

4. All Nazi laws which provided the basis of the Hitler regime or established discriminations on grounds of race, creed, or political opinion shall be abolished. No such discriminations, whether legal, administrative or otherwise, shall be tolerated.

5. War criminals and those who have participated in planning or carrying out Nazi enterprises involving or resulting in atrocities or war crimes shall be arrested and brought to judgment. . . .

6. All members of the Nazi Party who have been more than nominal participants in its activities and all other persons hostile to Allied purposes shall be removed from public and semi-public office, and from positions of responsibility in important private undertakings. . . .

7. German education shall be so controlled as completely to eliminate Nazi and militarist doctrines and to make possible the successful development of democratic ideas.

8. The judicial system will be reorganized in accordance with the principles of democracy, of justice under law, and of equal rights for all citizens without distinction of race, nationality or religion.

9. The administration in Germany should be directed towards the decentralization of the political structure and the development of local responsibility. . . . For the time being, no central German Government shall be established. . . .

10. Subject to the necessity for maintaining military security, freedom of speech, press and religion shall be permitted, and religious institutions shall be respected. Subject likewise to the maintenance of military security, the formation of free trade unions shall be permitted.

B. Economic Principles

11. In order to eliminate Germany's war potential, the production of arms, ammunition and implements of war as well as all types of aircraft and sea-going ships shall be prohibited and prevented. Production of metals, chemicals, machinery and other items that are directly necessary to a war economy shall be rigidly controlled and

restricted to Germany's approved post-war peacetime needs. . . .

12. At the earliest practicable date, the German economy shall be decentralized for the purpose of eliminating the present excessive concentration of economic power as exemplified in particular by cartels, syndicates, trusts and other monopolistic arrangements.

13. In organizing the German economy, primary emphasis shall be given to the development of agriculture and peaceful domestic industries.

14. During the period of occupation Germany shall be treated as a single economic unit. . . .

15. Allied controls shall be imposed upon the German economy but only to the extent necessary:

(a) to carry out programs of industrial disarmament, demilitarization, of reparations, and of approved exports and imports.

(b) to assure the production and maintenance of goods and services required to meet the needs of the occupying forces and displaced persons in Germany and essential to maintain in Germany average living standards not exceeding the average of the standards of living of European countries. . . .

— 63 —

CHARTER OF THE TRIBUNAL FOR THE TRIAL OF WAR CRIMINALS, AUGUST 8, 1945[1]

More than one Allied conference had promised that war criminals would be tried at the end of the war, and

[1] From *Department of State Bulletin*, XIII, No. 320 (Aug. 12, 1945), pp. 223-226.

immediately after the Potsdam conference agreement was reached in London on the establishment of a military tribunal for Europe. A notable feature of the tribunal's charter was the listing of crimes against peace and humanity, as well as conventional war crimes, as falling within the tribunal's jurisdiction. The General Assembly of the United Nations on December 11, 1946 affirmed the principles of the charter to be consonant with international law.

✓   ✓   ✓

II. JURISDICTION AND GENERAL PRINCIPLES.

ARTICLE VI.

The Tribunal . . . shall have the power to try and punish persons who, acting in the interests of the European Axis countries, whether as individuals or as members of organizations, committed any of the following crimes.

(a) CRIMES AGAINST PEACE: namely, planning, preparation, initiation or waging of a war of aggression, or a war in violation of international treaties, agreements or assurances, or participation in a common plan or conspiracy for the accomplishment of any of the foregoing;

(b) WAR CRIMES: namely, violations of the laws or customs of war. Such violations shall include, but not be limited to, murder, ill-treatment or deportation to slave labor or for any other purpose of civilian population of or in occupied territory, murder or ill-treatment of prisoners of war or persons on the seas, killing of hostages, plunder of public or private property, wanton destruction of cities, towns or villages, or devastation not justified by military necessity;

(c) CRIMES AGAINST HUMANITY: namely, murder, extermination, enslavement, deportation, and other inhumane acts committed against any civilian population, before or during the war; or persecutions on political, racial or religious grounds in execution of or in connection with any crime within the jurisdiction of the Tribunal, whether or not in violation of the domestic law of the country where perpetrated. . . .

64

UNITED STATES PROPOSALS FOR THE INTERNATIONAL CONTROL OF ATOMIC POWER, JUNE 14, 1946[1]

With a sense of responsibility for having unleashed atomic power, the United States government took the lead in seeking to subject its destructive uses to international control. On November 15, 1945, the United States, joined by Great Britain and Canada, called on the United Nations to take the initiative to this end; and in January, 1946, the United Nations Assembly, at its first meeting, established an Atomic Energy Commission. Two months later the Acheson-Lilienthal report developed the basic control program which was embodied in the far-reaching proposals Mr. Baruch laid before the Commission in June. This summary appeared in the United Nations Bulletin.

⟋   ⟋   ⟋

. . . . At the Commission's first meeting in New York on June 14, the representative of the United States, Bernard M. Baruch, submitted a United States plan based on the establishment of an International Atomic Development Authority entrusted with all phases of the development and use of atomic energy.

He stressed the fundamental importance of immediate punishment for infringements of the rights of this Authority, and stated that, accordingly, "there must be no veto to protect those who violate their solemn agreements

[1] From *United Nations Weekly Bulletin,* I (Aug. 26, 1946), No. 4, pp. 2-3.

not to develop or use atomic energy for destructive purposes."

. . . The plan contains the following specific proposals:

1. The Authority should conduct continuous surveys of world supplies of uranium and thorium and bring the raw materials under its dominion.

2. The Authority should control and operate all of the primary production plants producing fissionable products in dangerous quantities, and all plants dealing with uranium or thorium after it has once reached the potential of dangerous use.

3. The Authority should possess the exclusive right to conduct research in the field of atomic explosives, and all other atomic research should be open only to nations under license of the Authority, which would furnish them with denatured materials.

4. Dangerous activities of the Authority and its stockpiles should be decentralized and strategically distributed.

5. Freedom for any inspection deemed necessary by the Authority should be granted by nations.

The representative of the United States proposed that, once renunciation of the bomb as a weapon had been agreed upon and an adequate system of control put into effective operation, with punishments set up for any violations, manufacture of atomic bombs should stop, existing bombs should be disposed of under treaty, and the Authority should be given full information as to the know-how for atomic energy production. Subject to constitutional approval, the United States Government would make available to the Authority, at successive stages specified in the charter of the Authority, the information necessary for its effective functioning at each of these stages in its progressive assumption of control.

65

THE TRUMAN DOCTRINE, MARCH 12, 1947[1]

By the beginning of 1947, the United States and Soviet Union had reached a stalemate on the major problems that required their agreement, but this set no limit on Russian expansion. Soviet power was entrenched in eastern Europe, but Greece and Turkey blocked Russia's way to the Mediterranean and the Middle East. When Great Britain informed the United States in February that it could no longer bolster up Greece with troops or continue financial aid to either Greece or Turkey, President Truman decided to take over Britain's historic role in this area. From this limited strategic decision, the President went on to promise American aid to any peoples whose independence was threatened by totalitarianism. This was in effect a policy of containment since the United States was offering to prevent the further spread of Soviet domination.

᛬   ᛬   ᛬

PRESIDENT TRUMAN'S ADDRESS TO CONGRESS

The gravity of the situation which confronts the world today necessitates my appearance before a joint session of the Congress. . . .

The United States has received from the Greek Government an urgent appeal for financial and economic assistance. . . .

The very existence of the Greek state is today threatened by the terrorist activities of several thousand armed men, led by Communists, who defy the Government's authority at a number of points. . . . Meanwhile, the

[1] From *Department of State Bulletin*, XVI, No. 409A (Supplement, May 4, 1947), pp. 829-832.

Greek Government is unable to cope with the situation. The Greek Army is small and poorly equipped. It needs supplies and equipment if it is to restore authority to the Government throughout Greek territory. . . .

We have considered how the United Nations might assist in this crisis. But the situation is an urgent one requiring immediate action, and the United Nations and its related organizations are not in a position to extend help of the kind that is required. . . .

Greece's neighbor, Turkey, also deserves our attention.

The future of Turkey as an independent and economically sound state is clearly no less important to the freedom-loving peoples of the world than the future of Greece . . . Since the war Turkey has sought additional financial assistance from Great Britain and the United States for the purpose of effecting that modernization necessary for the maintenance of its national integrity. That integrity is essential to the preservation of order in the Middle East. The British Government has informed us that, owing to its own difficulties, it can no longer extend financial or economic aid to Turkey. . . .

I am fully aware of the broad implications involved if the United States extends assistance to Greece and Turkey, and I shall discuss these implications with you at this time.

One of the primary objectives of the foreign policy of the United States is the creation of conditions in which we and other nations will be able to work out a way of life free from coercion. . . . To insure the peaceful development of nations, free from coercion, the United States has taken a leading part in establishing the United Nations. The United Nations is designed to make possible lasting freedom and independence for all its members. We shall not realize our objectives, however, unless we are willing to help free peoples to maintain their free institutions and their national integrity against aggressive movements that seek to impose upon them totalitarian regimes. . . .

The peoples of a number of countries of the world have recently had totalitarian regimes forced upon them against their will. The Government of the United States has made frequent protests against coercion and intimidation, in violation of the Yalta agreement, in Poland, Rumania, and Bulgaria. . . .

I believe that it must be the policy of the United States to support free peoples who are resisting attempted subjugation by armed minorities or by outside pressures. . . .

The world is not static, and the *status quo* is not sacred. But we can not allow changes in the *status quo* in violation of the Charter of the United Nations by such methods as coercion, or by such subterfuges as political infiltration. In helping free and independent nations to maintain their freedom, the United States will be giving effect to the principles of the Charter of the United Nations. . . .

I therefore ask the Congress to provide authority for assistance to Greece and Turkey in the amount of $400,-000,000 for the period ending June 30, 1948 . . . to authorize the detail of American civilian and military personnel to Greece and Turkey, at the request of those countries, to assist in the tasks of reconstruction, and for the purpose of supervising the use of such financial and material assistance as may be furnished. I recommend that authority also be provided for the instruction and training of selected Greek and Turkish personnel. . . .

— 66 —

THE CASE FOR CONTAINMENT JULY, 1947[1]

In 1947 after many years in the Foreign Service, George F. Kennan was given responsibility for organizing

[1] From (George F. Kennan), "The Sources of Soviet Conduct," *Foreign Affairs*, XXV, No. 4 (July, 1947), pp. 566-582.

and directing a Policy Planning Staff for United States foreign relations. For this reason Mr. Kennan did not sign his article, "The Sources of Soviet Conduct," which appeared in the quarterly, Foreign Affairs, in July. Once described as "the most learned of our officials, the most experienced of our scholars," Mr. Kennan here points to weaknesses in the Soviet system which might prove fatal if the Soviet Union were everywhere checked by a firm policy of containment. It is to be noted that President Truman had already inaugurated such a policy in asking Congress for aid for Greece and Turkey. Mr. Kennan wrote before the Soviet Union had the atomic bomb and before communism had possessed China.

↗   ↗   ↗

. . . . The Soviet pressure against the free institutions of the western world is something that can be contained by the adroit and vigilant application of counter-force at a series of constantly shifting geographical and political points, corresponding to the shifts and maneuvers of Soviet policy, but which cannot be charmed or talked out of existence. The Russians look forward to a duel of infinite duration, and they see that already they have scored great successes. . . .

But if ideology convinces the rulers of Russia that truth is on their side and that they can therefore afford to wait, those of us on whom that ideology has no claim are free to examine objectively the validity of that premise. The Soviet thesis not only implies complete lack of control by the West over its own economic destiny, it likewise assumes Russian unity, discipline and patience over an infinite period. Let us bring this apocalyptic vision down to earth, and suppose that the western world finds the strength and resourcefulness to contain Soviet power over a period of ten to fifteen years. What does that spell for Russia itself?

The Soviet leaders, taking advantage of the contributions of modern technique to the arts of despotism, have solved the question of obedience within the confines of their power. Few challenge their authority; and even those who do are unable to make that challenge valid as against the organs of suppression of the state.

The Kremlin has also proved able to accomplish its

purpose of building up in Russia, regardless of the interests of the inhabitants, an industrial foundation of heavy metallurgy, which is, to be sure, not yet complete but which is nevertheless continuing to grow and is approaching those of the other major industrial countries. All of this, however, both the maintenance of internal political security and the building of heavy industry, has been carried out at a terrible cost in human life and in human hopes and energies. . . .

To all that, the war has added its tremendous toll of destruction, death and human exhaustion. In consequence of this, we have in Russia today a population which is physically and spiritually tired. The mass of the people are disillusioned, skeptical and no longer as accessible as they once were to the magical attraction which Soviet power still radiates to its followers abroad. . . .

In these circumstances, there are limits to the physical and nervous strength of people themselves. These limits are absolute ones, and are binding even for the cruelest dictatorship, because beyond them people cannot be driven. The forced labor camps and the other agencies of constraint provide temporary means of compelling people to work longer hours than their own volition or mere economic pressure would dictate; but if people survive them at all they become old before their time and must be considered as human casualties to the demands of dictatorship. In either case their best powers are no longer available to society and can no longer be enlisted in the service of the state.

Here only the younger generation can help. The younger generation, despite all vicissitudes and sufferings, is numerous and vigorous; and the Russians are a talented people. But it still remains to be seen what will be the effects on mature performance of the abnormal emotional strains of childhood which Soviet dictatorship created and which were enormously increased by the war. . . .

In addition to this, we have the fact that Soviet economic development, while it can list certain formidable achievements, has been precariously spotty and uneven. . . .

It is difficult to see how these deficiencies can be corrected at an early date by a tired and dispirited population working largely under the shadow of fear and com-

pulsion. And as long as they are not overcome, Russia
will remain economically a vulnerable, and in a certain
sense an impotent, nation, capable of exporting its en-
thusiasms and of radiating the strange charm of its primitive political vitality but unable to back up those articles
of export by the real evidences of material power and
prosperity.

Meanwhile, a great uncertainty hangs over the political
life of the Soviet Union. That is the uncertainty involved
in the transfer of power from one individual or group of
individuals to others.

This is, of course, outstandingly the problem of the
personal position of Stalin. We must remember that his
succession to Lenin's pinnacle of preeminence in the
Communist movement was the only such transfer of individual authority which the Soviet Union has experienced. That transfer took twelve years to consolidate. It
cost the lives of millions of people and shook the state to
its foundations, the attendant tremors were felt all
through the international revolutionary movement, to the
disadvantage of the Kremlin itself. . . .

But this is not only a question of Stalin himself. There
has been, since 1938, a dangerous congealment of political life in the higher circles of Soviet power. . . . The
same small group of men has carried on at the top
through an amazing series of national vicissitudes. . . .

Who can say whether, in these circumstances, the
eventual rejuvenation of the higher spheres of authority
(which can only be a matter of time) can take place
smoothly and peacefully, or whether rivals in the quest
for higher power will not eventually reach down into
these politically immature and inexperienced masses in
order to find support for their respective claims. If this
were ever to happen, strange consequences could flow
for the Communist Party: for the membership at large
has been exercised only in the practices of iron discipline
and obedience and not in the arts of compromise and ac-
commodation. And if disunity were ever to seize and
paralyze the Party, the chaos and weakness of Russian
society would be revealed in forms beyond description.
For we have seen that Soviet power is only a crust con-
cealing an amorphous mass of human beings among

whom no independent organizational structure is tolerated. . . .

Thus the future of Soviet power may not be by any means as secure as Russian capacity for self-delusion would make it appear to the men in the Kremlin. . . . Who can say with assurance that the strong light still cast by the Kremlin on the dissatisfied peoples of the western world is not the powerful afterglow of a constellation which is in actuality on the wane? . . . .

It is clear that the United States cannot expect in the foreseeable future to enjoy political intimacy with the Soviet regime. It must continue to regard the Soviet Union as a rival, not a partner, in the political arena. It must continue to expect that Soviet policies will reflect no abstract love of peace and stability, no real faith in the possibility of a permanent happy coexistence of the socialist and capitalist worlds, but rather a cautious, persistent pressure toward the disruption and weakening of all rival influence and rival power.

Balanced against this are the facts that Russia, as opposed to the western world in general, is still by far the weaker party, that Soviet policy is highly flexible, and that Soviet society may well contain deficiencies which will eventually weaken its own total potential. This would of itself warrant the United States entering with reasonable confidence upon a policy of firm containment, designed to confront the Russians with unalterable counterforce at every point where they show signs of encroaching upon the interests of a peaceful and stable world.

But in actuality the possibilities for American policy are by no means limited to holding the line and hoping for the best. It is entirely possible for the United States to influence by its actions the internal developments, both within Russia and throughout the international Communist movement, by which Russian policy is largely determined. . . .

It would be an exaggeration to say that American behavior unassisted and alone could exercise a power of life and death over the Communist movement and bring about the early fall of Soviet power in Russia. But the United States has it in its power to increase enormously the strains under which Soviet policy must operate, to force upon the Kremlin a far greater degree of moderation and circumspection than it has had to observe in recent years, and in this way to promote tendencies which must eventually find their outlet in either the break-up or the gradual mellowing of Soviet power. For no mystical, Messianic movement—and particularly not that of the Kremlin—can face frustration indefinitely without eventually adjusting itself in one way or another to the logic of that state of affairs. . . .

— 67 —

THE MARSHALL PLAN, NOVEMBER 10, 1947[1]

Speaking at the Harvard commencement on June 5, 1947, Secretary of State George C. Marshall announced the willingness of the United States to contribute to European recovery on the basis of a plan that promised "a cure rather than a mere palliative." The United States had already contributed heavily for relief on a piecemeal basis, but the European economy remained on dead center, and communism was feeding on the "hunger, poverty, desperation and chaos" General Marshall designated as the common enemy. The offer of American aid was denounced by Russia, but sixteen nations outside the Soviet sphere responded eagerly and by September had formulated a four-year plan of European recovery on the assumption of substantial assistance from the United States. After debate of almost three months, Congress passed the administration's European Recovery Program by large majorities. This statement was made by Secretary Marshall before a joint session of the Senate Com-

[1] From Senate Committee on Foreign Relations, *A Decade of American Foreign Policy* (Washington, 1950), pp. 1270-1277.

mittee on Foreign Relations and the House Committee on Foreign Affairs.

✓   ✓   ✓

. . . The President will lay before the Congress the program of his administration for aid to Europe. My duty as Secretary of State is to present the reasons for this program; the reasons why I profoundly believe that the vital interest of the United States is directly involved. . . .

As a result of the war, the European community which for centuries had been one of the most productive and indeed creative portions of the inhabited world was left prostrate. . . .

All the nations of Europe, 16 in number, which were in a position to exercise free choice gave a prompt and energetic response to the simple suggestion made at Harvard on June 5 last and thereby an impressive demonstration of the continuing vitality of European civilization.

It would be well, therefore, to deal briefly with what the area encompassed by those 16 nations plus western Germany has meant to us and has meant to the world. This community before the war accounted for nearly one-half of the world's trade. They owned nearly two-thirds of the world's shipping. Their industrial production in terms of the basic commodities of coal, steel, and chemicals was before the war slightly greater than that of the United States. Their economy was highly integrated, each part depending upon the efficient working of the others. . . .

The Committee of European Economic Cooperation, meeting in Paris, produced a recovery program extending over 4 years. After the most careful checking, with the assistance of experts drawn from many governmental agencies, we have concluded that the Paris report correctly identifies the courses of action necessary to produce recovery and indicates an approximate order of magnitude of the cost for the full 4-year program. On the basis of present indications, the estimated cost to our Treasury of this program may be of the order of magnitude of 16 to 20 billion dollars. . . .

I do not have to tell you that this foreign economic program of the United States seeks no special advantage and pursues no sinister purpose. It is a program of construction, production, and recovery. It menaces no one. It is designed specifically to bring to an end in the shortest possible time the dependence of these countries upon aid from the United States. We wish to see them self-supporting. . . .

The automatic success of the program cannot be guaranteed. The imponderables are many. The risks are real. They are, however, risks which have been carefully calculated, and I believe the chances of success are good. There is convincing evidence that the peoples of western Europe want to preserve their free society and the heritage we share with them. To make that choice conclusive they need our assistance. . . .

We must not fail to meet this inspiring challenge. We must not permit the free community of Europe to be extinguished. Should this occur it would be a tragedy for the world. It would impose incalculable burdens upon this country and force serious readjustments in our traditional way of life. One of our important freedoms—freedom of choice in both domestic and foreign affairs—would be drastically curtailed.

Whether we like it or not, we find ourselves, our Nation, in a world position of vast responsibility. We can act for our own good by acting for the world's good.

— 68 —

THE VANDENBERG RESOLUTION, JUNE 11, 1948 [1]

As the cold war intensified, the Truman administration became increasingly aware of the defenselessness of west-

[1] From *The Private Papers of Senator Vandenberg,* eds., Arthur H. Vandenberg, Jr., and Joe Alex Morris (Boston, 1952), p. 407. Copyright of Houghton Mifflin Co., Boston.

ern Europe. In March, 1948, Great Britain, France and the Benelux countries, with similar concern, signed a fifty-year defensive alliance at Brussels. President Truman at once addressed Congress on the significance of this move and stressed the importance of helping the Brussels pact nations "to protect themselves." About this time Senator Vandenberg began working on the problem of European security. A pre-war isolationist, he had become a strong advocate of the United Nations; and he now sought a scheme of western defense "within the charter but outside the veto." The Vandenberg resolution, passed by the Senate 64 to 6, gave the State Department advance approval of the historic commitment made the following year in the North Atlantic Treaty.

Whereas peace with justice and the defense of human rights and fundamental freedoms require international cooperation through more effective use of the United Nations: therefore be it

Resolved, that the Senate reaffirm the policy of the United States to achieve international peace and security through the United Nations so that armed force shall not be used except in the common interest, and that the President be advised of the sense of the Senate that this government, by constitutional process, should particularly pursue the following objectives within the United Nations Charter:

(1) Voluntary agreement to remove the veto from all questions involving pacific settlements of international disputes and situations, and from the admission of new members.

(2) Progressive development of regional and other collective arrangements for individual and collective self-defense in accordance with the purposes, principles, and provisions of the Charter.

(3) Association of the United States by constitutional process, with such regional and other collective arrangements as are based on continuous and effective self-help and mutual aid, and as affect its national security.

(4) Contributing to the maintenance of peace by making clear its determination to exercise the right of individual or collective self-defense under Article 51 should

any armed attack occur affecting its national security.

(5) Maximum efforts to obtain agreements to provide the United Nations with armed forces as provided by the Charter, and to obtain agreement among member nations upon universal regulation and reduction of armaments under adequate and dependable guaranty against violation.

(6) If necessary, after adequate effort toward strengthening the United Nations, review of the Charter at an appropriate time by a General Conference called under Article 109 or by the General Assembly.

— 69 —

BERLIN BLOCKADE AND AIRLIFT, 1948-1949[1]

While Congress was debating the European Recovery Program, the Soviet Union added Czechoslovakia to its domain by a Communist coup at Prague in February, 1948. In the following April the Russians began a campaign to force the western Powers out of Berlin which lay deep in the Soviet zone of Germany. By June all water, rail and highway routes were closed between Berlin and the western zones. President Truman here interprets the meaning of the Soviet blockade of Berlin and tells of the decision to maintain the Allied position in the city at all costs. The spectacular success of the airlift led to a Soviet agreement to end the blockade in May, 1949.

✓   ✓   ✓

. . . What was at stake in Berlin was not a contest

[1] From *Memoirs by Harry S. Truman*, II, pp. 123-126. Copyright of Time, Inc., N. Y.

over legal rights, although our position was entirely sound in international law, but a struggle over Germany and, in a larger sense, over Europe. In the face of our launching of the Marshall Plan, the Kremlin tried to mislead the people of Europe into believing that our interest and support would not extend beyond economic matters and that we would back away from any military risks.

I brought up the situation at the Cabinet meeting of June 25. Secretary of the Army Kenneth Royall maintained constant touch with General Clay in Germany and reported that a serious situation was developing. . . . Clay was forced to make emergency arrangements to have essential supplies flown into the city, since Berlin, by now, was effectively blockaded by the Russians both by land and by water.

On June 26, the day after I discussed the Berlin crisis with the Cabinet, I directed that this improvised "airlift" be put on a full-scale organized basis and that every plane available to our European Command be impressed into service. . . .

General Clay came to the White House on July 22, 1948, to attend the meeting that day of the National Security Council, and I asked him to report on the situation in Germany.

Here, in substance, is what he said: The abandonment of Berlin would have a disastrous effect upon our plans for Western Germany. It would also slow down European recovery, the success of which depended upon more production, particularly from Western Germany. The Germans in general were more concerned than the Allies about the possibility of our leaving Berlin. We should be prepared to go to any lengths to find a peaceful solution to the situation, but we had to remain in Berlin.

The attitude of the German people, Clay added, was in some respects unbelievable. The party leaders in Berlin who made up the City Magistrate, with headquarters in the Soviet zone, had absolutely refused to accept Soviet control. The people of Berlin were determined to stand firm even if it required undergoing additional hardships.

He reported that the airlift had been averaging about 2,400 to 2,500 tons per day, which was more than enough to handle food requirements, but was inadequate to include the necessary amounts of coal. The minimum required to sustain Berlin without extreme hardship was estimated at 4,500 tons per day. . . .

I then asked General Clay what risks would be involved if we tried to supply Berlin by means of armed convoys. The general said he thought the initial reaction of the Russians would be to set up road blocks. Our engineers would be able to clear such obstacles, provided there was no Russian interference, but the next step the Russians would take, General Clay thought, would be to meet the convoys with armed force.

Robert Lovett, who was in attendance with Secretary Marshall, asked Clay if he thought the Russians might try to block our airplanes with fighter patrols or by other methods. General Clay said he felt that the Russians would not attack our planes unless they had made the decision to go to war.

I asked General Clay if there were any indications known to him that the Russians would go to war. He said he did not think so. What they seemed to be aiming at was to score a major victory by forcing us out of Berlin, either now or after fall and winter weather forced us to curtail the airlift, without, however, extending the conflict.

We discussed the kind of assistance that we might expect from our allies if the conflict became more intense. I stated it as my judgment that if we moved out of Berlin we would be losing everything we were fighting for. The main question was: How could we remain in Berlin without risking all-out war?

General Vandenberg said again that he felt the concentration of aircraft necessary to provide Berlin with all its supplies by air would mean reducing our air strength elsewhere, both in planes and in personnel. An emergency would find us more exposed than we might be able to afford.

I did not agree with the Air Force Chief of Staff. I asked him if he would prefer to have us attempt to supply Berlin by ground convoy. Then, if the Russians resisted that effort and plunged the world into war, would not the Air Force have to contribute its share to the defense of the nation? I answered my own question: The airlift involved less risks than armed road convoys.

Therefore, I directed the Air Force to furnish the fullest support possible to the problem of supplying Berlin. . . .

— 70 —

THE POINT FOUR PROGRAM, JANUARY 20, 1949[1]

In his inaugural address President Truman listed four points in his program for "peace and freedom." The first three pledged the United States to support of the United Nations, the continuance of programs of economic recovery abroad, and assistance to nations threatened with aggression. From the fourth point evolved, in due course, an extensive if thin network of technical assistance to non-Communist countries.

. . . Fourth, we must embark on a bold new program for making the benefits of our scientific advances and industrial progress available for the improvement and growth of undeveloped areas.

More than half the people of the world are living in conditions approaching misery. Their food is inadequate. They are victims of disease. Their economic life is primitive and stagnant. Their poverty is a handicap and a threat both to them and to more prosperous areas. . . .

I believe that we should make available to peace-loving peoples the benefits of our store of technical knowledge in order to help them realize their aspirations for a better life. And, in cooperation with other nations, we should

[1] From *Department of State Bulletin*, XX, No. 500 (Jan. 30, 1949), pp. 123-126.

foster capital investment in areas needing development. . . .

With the cooperation of business, private capital, agriculture, and labor in this country, this program can
greatly increase the industrial activity in other nations
and can raise substantially their standards of living. . . .

The old imperialism—exploitation for foreign profit—
has no place in our plans. What we envisage is a program
of development based on the concepts of democratic fair-
dealing.

All countries, including our own, will greatly benefit
from a constructive program for the better use of the
world's human and natural resources. Experience shows
that our commerce with other countries expands as they
progress industrially and economically. . . .

Democracy alone can supply the vitalizing force to
stir the peoples of the world into triumphant action, not
only against their human oppressors, but also against
their ancient enemies—hunger, misery, and despair. . . .

— 71 —

NORTH ATLANTIC TREATY, APRIL 4, 1949[1]

*The ambitious scheme of regional security known as
NATO had its origins in the Brussels alliance and in the
decision of the Truman administration of July 2, 1948,
to join in the defense of western Europe, even at the
cost of "entangling alliances." Signed on April 4, 1949, the
North Atlantic Treaty was approved by the Senate 82 to
13 on July 21, and sufficient ratifications had been made
by the twelve member states to give the treaty organiza-*

[1] From United Nations, *Treaty Series,* 33 (1949) pp. 243-255.

*tion official existence on August 24. Membership in the
North Atlantic Treaty Organization committed the United
States to go to the defense of European states in Europe
and to contribute to NATO's "collective strength" to resist attack. On April 4, 1951, exactly two years after the
treaty's ceremonial signing, the Senate approved the
President's proposal to send four divisions to Europe, in
addition to two already there, for the new NATO army,
while reserving the right of Congress to be consulted
about additional forces. At the same time the Senate endorsed the appointment of General Eisenhower as the
first Supreme Commander of NATO forces.*

The Parties to this Treaty reaffirm their faith in the
purposes and principles of the Charter of the United
Nations and their desire to live in peace with all peoples
and all governments.

They are determined to safeguard the freedom, common
heritage and civilization of their peoples, founded on the
principles of democracy, individual liberty and the rule of
law.

They seek to promote stability and well-being in the
North Atlantic area.

They are resolved to unite their efforts for collective
defense and for the preservation of peace and security.

They therefore agree to this North Atlantic Treaty:

ARTICLE 1. The Parties undertake, as set forth in the
Charter of the United Nations, to settle any international
disputes in which they may be involved by peaceful
means. . . .

ARTICLE 2. The Parties will contribute toward the
further development of peaceful and friendly international relations by strengthening their free institutions,
by bringing about a better understanding of the principles
upon which these institutions are founded, and by promoting conditions of stability and well-being. They will
seek to eliminate conflict in their international economic
policies and will encourage economic collaboration between any or all of them.

ARTICLE 3. In order more effectively to achieve the
objectives of this Treaty, the Parties, separately and
jointly, by means of continuous and effective self-help

and mutual aid, will maintain and develop their individual and collective capacity to resist armed attack.

ARTICLE 4. The Parties will consult together whenever, in the opinion of any of them, the territorial integrity, political independence or security of any of the Parties is threatened.

ARTICLE 5. The Parties agree that an armed attack against one or more of them in Europe or North America shall be considered an attack against them all; and consequently they agree that, if such an armed attack occurs, each of them, in exercise of the right of individual or collective self-defense recognized by Article 51 of the Charter of the United Nations, will assist the Party or Parties so attacked by taking forthwith, individually and in concert with the other Parties, such action as it deems necessary, including the use of armed force, to restore and maintain the security of the North Atlantic area. . . .

ARTICLE 6. For the purpose of Article 5 an armed attack on one or more of the Parties is deemed to include an armed attack on the territory of any of the Parties in Europe or North America, on the Algerian departments of France, on the occupation forces of any Party in Europe, on the islands under the jurisdiction of any Party in the North Atlantic area north of the Tropic of Cancer or on the vessels or aircraft in this area of any of the Parties.

ARTICLE 7. This Treaty does not affect, and shall not be interpreted as affecting, in any way the rights and obligations under the Charter of the Parties which are members of the United Nations, or the primary responsibility of the Security Council for the maintenance of international peace and security.

ARTICLE 8. Each Party declares that none of the international engagements now in force between it and any other of the Parties or any third State is in conflict with the provisions of this Treaty, and undertakes not to enter into any international engagement in conflict with this Treaty.

ARTICLE 9. The Parties hereby establish a council, on which each of them shall be represented, to consider matters concerning the implementation of this Treaty. The council shall be so organized as to be able to meet promptly at any time. The council shall set up such sub-sidiary bodies as may be necessary; in particular it shall establish immediately a defense committee which shall recommend measures for the implementation of Articles 3 and 5.

ARTICLE 10. The Parties may, by unanimous agreement, invite any other European state in a position to further the principles of this Treaty and to contribute to the security of the North Atlantic area to accede to this Treaty. . . .

— 72 —

THREE POWER STATEMENT ON ARMING ISRAEL AND THE ARAB STATES AND DEFENDING THE STATUS QUO, MAY 25, 1950[1]

In spite of the armistice which the United Nations succeeded in negotiating, hostilities between the new state of Israel and adjacent Arab states continued in border raids and in the blockade of Israel by land, pipe-line, and Suez canal. The problem of Palestinian Arab refugees remained unsolved and both sides sought arms for the expected resumption of full-scale war. The United States was eager to end the Arab-Israeli feud so that the whole Middle East area might be organized against Soviet penetration; but, as an interim measure, it joined

[1] From *Department of State Bulletin,* XXII, No. 570 (June 5, 1950), p. 886.

Britain and France in rationing arms to states taking the pledge against aggression and promising assistance to any state in the area that was attacked by its neighbor.

✓   ✓   ✓

The Governments of the United Kingdom, France, and the United States, having had occasion during the recent Foreign Ministers' meeting in London to review certain questions affecting the peace and stability of the Arab states and of Israel, and particularly that of the supply of arms and war materials to these states, have resolved to make the following statement:

1. The three Governments recognize that the Arab states and Israel all need to maintain a certain level of armed forces for the purposes of assuring their internal security and their legitimate self-defense and to permit them to play their part in the defense of the area as a whole. All applications for arms or war materials for these countries will be considered in the light of these principles. In this connection the three Governments wish to recall and reaffirm the terms of the statements made by their representatives on the Security Council on August 4, 1949, in which they declared their opposition to the development of an arms race between the Arab states and Israel.

2. The three Governments declare that assurances have been received from all the states in question, to which they permit arms to be supplied from their countries, that the purchasing state does not intend to undertake any act of aggression against any other state. Similar assurances will be requested from any other state in the area to which they permit arms to be supplied in the future.

3. The three Governments take this opportunity of declaring their deep interest in and their desire to promote the establishment and maintenance of peace and stability in the area and their unalterable opposition to the use of force or threat of force between any of the states in that area. The three Governments, should they find that any of these states was preparing to violate frontiers or armistice lines, would, consistently with their obligations as members of the United Nations, immediately take ac-

tion, both within and outside the United Nations, to prevent such violation.

— 73 —

TRUMAN ON THE DEFENSE OF SOUTH KOREA, JUNE 27, 1950[1]

On January 12, 1950, Secretary of State Acheson stated that the United States defensive perimeter ran from the Aleutians to Japan, then to the Ryukyus and on to the Philippines. Conspicuously omitted from his statement, Korea and Formosa lay beyond the bounds and, therefore, beyond any guaranty of American protection. Nevertheless, when North Korean troops invaded South Korea on June 25, 1950, President Truman in agreement with his military and diplomatic advisers decided to intervene with force to prevent a Communist victory. It is certain that the United States would have acted, whatever the United Nations did; but the Security Council, spared a veto by a timely Russian boycott, moved with despatch to stop aggression. The joint action in Korea, therefore, was a United Nations operation, although borne in great part by South Korea and the United States. At the same time, and independently of the United Nations, President Truman brought Formosa under American protection. The decisions on Korea and Formosa, announced by the President on June 27, revealed a determination to apply the policy of containment beyond the announced defense perimeter in the west Pacific.

✓   ✓   ✓

[1] From *Department of State Bulletin*, XXIII, No. 574 (July 3, 1950), p. 5.

STATEMENT BY THE PRESIDENT

In Korea, the Government forces, which were armed to prevent border raids and to preserve internal security, were attacked by invading forces from North Korea. The Security Council of the United Nations called upon the invading troops to cease hostilities and to withdraw to the 38th Parallel. This they have not done but, on the contrary, have pressed the attack. The Security Council called upon all members of the United Nations to render every assistance to the United Nations in the execution of this resolution. In these circumstances, I have ordered United States air and sea forces to give the Korean Government troops cover and support.

The attack upon Korea makes it plain beyond all doubt that communism has passed beyond the use of subversion to conquer independent nations and will now use armed invasion and war. It has defied the orders of the Security Council of the United Nations issued to preserve international peace and security. In these circumstances, the occupation of Formosa by Communist forces would be a direct threat to the security of the Pacific area and to United States forces performing their lawful and necessary functions in that area.

Accordingly, I have ordered the Seventh Fleet to prevent any attack on Formosa. As a corollary of this action, I am calling upon the Chinese Government on Formosa to cease all air and sea operations against the mainland. The Seventh Fleet will see that this is done. The determination of the future status of Formosa must await the restoration of security in the Pacific, a peace settlement with Japan, or consideration by the United Nations. . . .

I have similarly directed acceleration in the furnishing of military assistance to the forces of France and the Associated States in Indochina and the dispatch of a military mission to provide close working relations with those forces.

I know that all members of the United Nations will consider carefully the consequences of this latest aggression in Korea in defiance of the Charter of the United Nations. A return to the rule of force in international affairs would have far-reaching effects. The United States will continue to uphold the rule of law.

I have instructed Ambassador Austin, as the representative of the United States to the Security Council, to report these steps to the Council.

— 74 —

UNITING FOR PEACE, NOVEMBER 2, 1950[1]

Following the Security Council's brief term of energetic decision at the beginning of the Korean war, the Russian delegate returned and vetoed further action on Korea. On September 20, 1950, Secretary of State Acheson presented the United Nations General Assembly with a plan for halting aggression by action of the Assembly whenever the Security Council was paralyzed by disagreement between the permanent members. With the title, Uniting for Peace, the plan was adopted by a vote of 52 to 5 with two abstentions on November 2. At the same time the great powers were requested to meet with a view to resolving their "fundamental differences." Although hailed at the moment as a realistic solution of the veto impasse, the American device charged the Assembly with executive functions it was not designed to perform; and divisions within the Assembly, like those in the Security Council, could produce frustration and paralysis.

The General Assembly,

A.

1. Resolves that if the Security Council, because of lack of unanimity of the permanent members, fails to exercise

[1] From *United Nations Bulletin*, IX, No. 10 (Nov. 15, 1950), pp. 508-509.

its primary responsibility for the maintenance of international peace and security in any case where there appears to be a threat to the peace, breach of the peace, or act of aggression, the General Assembly shall consider the matter immediately with a view to making appropriate recommendations to Members for collective measures, including in the case of a breach of the peace or act of aggression the use of armed force when necessary, to maintain or restore international peace and security. . . .

B.

3. Establishes a Peace Observation Commission . . . which could observe and report on the situation in any area where there exists international tension the continuance of which is likely to endanger the maintenance of international peace and security. . . .

C.

7. Invites each Member of the United Nations to survey its resources in order to determine the nature and scope of the assistance it may be in a position to render in support of any recommendation of the Security Council or of the General Assembly for the restoration of international peace and security;

8. Recommends to the states Members of the United Nations that each Member maintain within its national armed forces elements so trained, organized, and equipped that they could promptly be made available, in accordance with its constitutional processes, for service as a United Nations unit or units, upon recommendation by the Security Council or General Assembly, without prejudice to the use of such elements in exercise of the right of individual or collective self-defence recognized in Article 51 of the Charter. . . .

75

AMERICAN-JAPANESE DEFENSE PACT SEPTEMBER 8, 1951[1]

Six years after Japan's surrender, a treaty of peace between forty-eight of the United Nations and Japan was signed in San Francisco on September 8, 1951. Between the surrender and the peace pact, American policy had done an about-face. At first Washington's objective was a democratic, unarmed Japan living at peace with its neighbors. When Communism added China to its domain and threatened further gains in east Asia, the American image of Japan changed to that of a well-armed ally. The early policy was embedded in the new Japanese Constitution which renounced war and ruled out armaments. The later policy is reflected in the peace treaty, which mentioned Japan's inherent right of individual and collective self-defense and its right to enter into collective security arrangements. The treaty marked the end of the occupation, but in a defense pact signed the same day, Japan granted the United States the right to maintain armed forces on Japanese territory as long as it chooses and to veto similar grants to a third power.

✦   ✦   ✦

TEXT OF THE TREATY

Japan has signed a Treaty of Peace with the Allied Powers. On the coming into force of that Treaty, Japan will not have the effective means to exercise its inherent right of self-defense because it has been disarmed. . . .

[1] From *Department of State Bulletin,* XXV, No. 638 (Sept. 17, 1951), pp. 464-465.

The Treaty of Peace recognizes that Japan as a sovereign nation has the right to enter into collective security arrangements, and, further, the Charter of the United Nations recognizes that all nations possess an inherent right of individual and collective self-defense.

In exercise of these rights, Japan desires, as a provisional arrangement for its defense, that the United States should maintain armed forces of its own in and about Japan so as to deter armed attack upon Japan.

The United States, in the interest of peace and security, is presently willing to maintain certain of its armed forces in and about Japan, in the expectation, however, that Japan will itself increasingly assume responsibility for its own defense against direct and indirect aggression. . . .

Accordingly the two countries have agreed as follows:

ARTICLE I. Japan grants, and the United States accepts the right, upon the coming into force of the Treaty of Peace and of this Treaty, to dispose United States land, air, and sea forces in and about Japan. Such forces may be utilized to contribute to the maintenance of international peace and security in the Far East and to the security of Japan against armed attack from without, including assistance given at the express request of the Japanese Government to put down large-scale internal riots and disturbances in Japan, caused through instigation or intervention by an outside Power or Powers.

ARTICLE II. During the exercise of the right referred to in Article I, Japan will not grant, without the prior consent of the United States, any bases or any rights, powers or authority whatsoever, in or relating to bases or the right of garrison or of maneuver, or transit of ground, air or naval forces to any third power.

ARTICLE III. The conditions which shall govern the disposition of armed forces of the United States in and about Japan shall be determined by administrative agreements between the two Governments.

ARTICLE IV. This Treaty shall expire whenever in the opinion of the Governments of the United States and of Japan there shall have come into force such United Nations arrangements or such alternate individual or collective security dispositions as will satisfactorily provide for the maintenance by the United Nations or otherwise of international peace and security in the Japan area. . . .

76

THE BATTLE ACT, OCTOBER 26, 1951[1]

*Twice during 1951 Congress implied criticism of the
Truman administration by enactments of policy relating
to East-West trade and foreign aid. The rider to an
appropriation bill ordered that no economic aid go to any
state which permitted strategic materials to go to Soviet-
dominated nations. President Truman protested the rider
but signed the bill on June 2, 1951. A sub-committee of
the House Committee on Foreign Affairs, under the chairmanship of Laurie C. Battle of Alabama, then designed a
bill which prescribed an American embargo against the
Soviet world and denied either economic or military aid
to any nation that refused to impose a like embargo.
Known as the Battle Act, this measure limited the element
of give-and-take in negotiation with other members of the
Western bloc, with neutrals, or with restive satellites.*

✓   ✓   ✓

MUTUAL DEFENSE ASSISTANCE
CONTROL ACT OF 1951

Section 101. The Congress of the United States, recognizing that in a world threatened by aggression the United
States can best preserve and maintain peace by developing
maximum national strength and by utilizing all of its
resources in cooperation with other free nations, hereby
declares it to be the policy of the United States to apply
an embargo on the shipment of arms, ammunition, and
implements of war, atomic energy materials, petroleum,
transportation materials of strategic value, and items of
primary strategic significance used in the production of
arms, ammunition and implements of war, to any nation

[1] From *United States Statutes at Large,* 1951, 65, pp. 644-647.

or combination of nations threatening the security of the United States, including the Union of Soviet Socialist Republics and all countries under its domination, in order to (1) increase the national strength of the United States and of the cooperating nations; (2) impede the ability of nations threatening the security of the United States to conduct military operations; and (3) to assist the people of the nations under the domination of foreign aggressors to reestablish their freedom.

It is further declared to be the policy of the United States that no military, economic, or financial assistance shall be supplied to any nation unless it applies an embargo on such shipments to any nation or combination of nations threatening the security of the United States, including the Union of Soviet Socialist Republics and all countries under its domination.

This Act shall be administered in such a way as to bring about the fullest support for any resolution of the General Assembly of the United Nations, supported by the United States, to prevent the shipment of certain commodities to areas under the control of governments engaged in hostilities in defiance of the United Nations. . . .

— 77 —

DEFENSE AGREEMENT WITH SPAIN, SEPTEMBER 26, 1953[1]

In disrepute as pro-Axis during World War II, and totalitarian by nature, Franco's Spain was not included in the North Atlantic Treaty whose preamble speaks well of "democracy, individual liberty and the rule of law." However, as NATO came into existence, United States military authorities stated their interest in airbases behind the Pyrenees, and four years later these were obtained

[1] From *Department of State Bulletin*, XXIX, No. 745 (Oct. 5, 1953), p. 436.

through a bi-lateral agreement with Spain. The defense agreement reprinted here was accompanied by two other pacts providing for arms and economic aid. The deal was denounced as fraternizing with and financing dictatorship and defended on strategic grounds.

✓   ✓   ✓

PREAMBLE. Faced with the danger that threatens the western world, the Governments of the United States and Spain, desiring to contribute to the maintenance of international peace and security through foresighted measures which will increase their capability and that of the other nations which dedicate their efforts to the same high purposes to participate effectively in agreements for self defense, Have agreed as follows:

ARTICLE I. In consonance with the principles agreed upon in the Mutual Defense Assistance Agreement, the Governments of the United States and of Spain consider that the contingencies with which both countries may be faced indicate the advisability of developing their relations upon a basis of continued friendship, in support of the policy of strengthening the defense of the West. This policy shall include:

1. On the part of the United States, the support of Spanish defense efforts for agreed purposes by providing military end item assistance to Spain during a period of several years to contribute to the effective air defense of Spain and to improve the equipment of its military and naval forces. . . .

2. In consequence of the above stated premises and for the same agreed purposes, the Government of Spain authorizes the Government of the United States, subject to terms and conditions to be agreed, to develop, maintain and utilize for military purposes, jointly with the Government of Spain, such areas and facilities in territory under Spanish jurisdiction as may be agreed upon. . . .

3. In granting assistance to Spain within the policy outlined above, as the preparation of the agreed areas and facilities progresses, the Government of the United States will satisfy, subject to the provisions of paragraph one, the minimum requirements for equipment necessary for

the defense of Spanish territory, to the end that should a moment requiring the wartime utilization of the areas and facilities arrive, from this moment, the requirements are covered to the extent possible as regards the air defense of the territory and the equipment of the naval units; and that the armament and equipment of the Army units be as far advanced as possible.

ARTICLE II. For the purposes of this agreement and in accordance with technical arrangements to be agreed upon between the competent authorities of both Governments, the Government of the United States is authorized to improve and fit agreed areas and facilities for military use, as well as to undertake necessary construction in this connection in cooperation with the Government of Spain, to station and house therein the necessary military and civilian personnel, and to provide for their security, discipline, and welfare. . . .

ARTICLE III. The areas which, by virtue of this Agreement, are prepared for joint utilization will remain under Spanish flag and command, and Spain will assume the obligation of adopting the necessary measures for the external security. However, the United States may, in all cases, exercise the necessary supervision of United States personnel, facilities, and equipment. . . .

— 78 —

ATOMS FOR PEACE: EISENHOWER'S PROPOSAL TO THE UNITED NATIONS, DECEMBER 8, 1953[1]

Year after year from 1946 the United Nations failed to reconcile the divergent positions of the United States and

[1] From *United Nations Bulletin*, XV, No. 12 (Dec. 15, 1953), pp. 555-557.

*Soviet Union on the international control of atomic
power. By 1953, when the two antagonists were both pre-
sumably producing hydrogen bombs of cataclysmic por-
tent, the need for control was greater than ever while the
prospect for agreement remained dim. In an address to
the General Assembly on December 8, 1953, President
Eisenhower proposed a modest plan for making atomic
energy available to all nations for peaceful purposes.
While the Eisenhower proposals left control mechanisms
to future deliberation, his plan had the peculiar merit of
satisfying everyone and a year later was unanimously
approved by the General Assembly.*

ᶜ   ᶜ   ᶜ

. . . I feel impelled to speak today in a language that
in a sense is new—one which I, who have spent so much
of my life in the military profession, would have pre-
ferred never to use.

That new language is the language of atomic warfare. . . .

Atomic bombs today are more than 25 times as powerful as the weapons with which the atomic age dawned,
while hydrogen weapons are in the ranges of millions of
tons of TNT equivalent.

Today, the United States' stockpile of atomic weapons,
which, of course, increases daily, exceeds by many times
the total equivalent of the total of all bombs and all shells
that came from every plane and every gun in every theatre
of war through all the years of World War II.

A single air group, whether afloat or land based, can
now deliver to any reachable target a destructive cargo
exceeding in power all of the bombs that fell on Britain
in all of World War II. . . .

If at one time the United States possessed what might
have been called a monopoly of atomic power, that monopoly ceased to exist several years ago. Therefore, although our earlier start has permitted us to accumulate
what is today a great quantitative advantage, the atomic
realities of today comprehend two facts of even greater
significance.

First, the knowledge now possessed by several nations
will eventually be shared by others, possibly all others.

Second, even a vast superiority in numbers of weapons

—and a consequent capability of devastating retaliation—is no preventive, of itself, against the fearful material damage and toll of human lives that would be inflicted by surprise aggression. . . .

Should such an atomic attack be launched against the United States, our reactions would be swift and resolute. But for me to say . . . that the retaliation capabilities of the United States are so great that such an aggressor's land would be laid waste—all this, while fact, is not the true expression of the purpose and the hope of the United States.

To pause there would be to confirm the hopeless finality of a belief that two atomic colossi are doomed malevolently to eye each other indefinitely across a trembling world. To stop there would be to accept helplessly the probability of civilization destroyed—the annihilation of the irreplaceable heritage of mankind handed down to us from generation to generation—and the condemnation of mankind to begin all over again the age-old struggle upward from savagery toward decency, right, and justice. . . .

My country wants to be constructive, not destructive. It wants agreements, not wars, among nations. It wants itself to live in freedom and in the confidence that the people of every nation enjoy equally the right of choosing their own way of life. . . .

The United States knows that if the fearful trend of atomic military buildup can be reversed, this greatest of destructive forces can be developed into a great boon, for the benefit of all mankind. . . .

To hasten the day when fear of the atom will begin to disappear from the minds of the people and the governments of the East and West, there are certain steps that can be taken now.

I therefore make the following proposal:

The Governments principally involved, to the extent permitted by elementary prudence, to begin now and continue to make joint contributions from their stockpiles of normal uranium and fissionable materials to an International Atomic Energy Agency. We would expect that such an agency would be set up under the aegis of the United Nations. . . .

I would be prepared to submit to the Congress of the

United States, and with every expectation of approval, any such plan that would:

First—encourage world-wide investigation into the most effective peacetime uses of fissionable material. . . .

Second—begin to diminish the potential destructive power of the world's atomic stockpiles;

Third—allow all peoples of all nations to see that, in this enlightened age, the great powers of the earth, both of the East and of the West, are interested in human aspirations first rather than in building up the armaments of war;

Fourth—open up a new channel for peaceful discussion and initiate at least a new approach to the many difficult problems that must be solved in both private and public conversations if the world is to shake off the inertia imposed by fear and make positive progress toward peace. . . .

The coming months will be fraught with fateful decisions. In this Assembly; in the capitals and military headquarters of the world; in the hearts of men everywhere, be they governed or governors—may they be the decisions which will lead this world out of fear and into peace.

To the making of these fateful decisions, the United States pledges before you—and therefore before the world —its determination to help solve the fearful atomic dilemma—to devote its entire heart and mind to find the way by which the miraculous inventiveness of man shall not be dedicated to his death, but consecrated to his life. . . .

PACIFIC CHARTER AND MANILA PACT, SEPTEMBER 8, 1954[1]

The idea of a security pact for the Pacific on the model of NATO had little serious support in Washington until the early summer of 1954 when the defeat of French forces in Indochina exposed the whole of southeast Asia to Communist penetration and conquest. Secretary of State Dulles sought to meet the threat through an organization of Asiatic states and interested western powers. Most of non-Communist Asia was committed to neutralism, and diplomatic or political considerations ruled out Japan, Nationalist China, and the states of Indochina. However Pakistan, Thailand and the Philippines were prepared to take a stand with the United States, Great Britain, France, Australia and New Zealand. Meeting in Manila, representatives of the eight states issued a Pacific Charter, emphasizing the right of self-determination, and signed a collective security treaty known as the Manila Pact. The commitment taken by each signatory falls short of that required by NATO, but for the United States the pact meant a further extension of obligation under the policy of containment. The Manila Pact grouping is often called SEATO, on the analogy of NATO, but it is too amorphous to be called an organization.

✦　　　✦　　　✦

THE PACIFIC CHARTER

The delegates of Australia, France, New Zealand, Pakistan, the Republic of the Philippines, the Kingdom of Thailand, the United Kingdom, the United States;

[1] From *Department of State Bulletin,* XXXI, No. 795 (Sept. 20, 1954), pp. 393-396.

Desiring to establish a firm basis for common action to maintain peace and security in Southeast Asia and the Southwest Pacific;

Convinced that common action to this end, in order to be worthy and effective, must be inspired by the highest principles of justice and liberty;

Do hereby proclaim:

First, in accordance with the provisions of the United Nations Charter, they uphold the principle of equal rights and self-determination of peoples and they will earnestly strive by every peaceful means to promote self-government and to secure the independence of all countries whose peoples desire it and are able to undertake its responsibilities;

Second, they are each prepared to continue taking effective measures to ensure conditions favorable to the orderly achievement of the foregoing purposes in accordance with their constitutional procedures;

Third, they will continue to cooperate in the economic, social and cultural fields in order to promote higher living standards, economic progress and social well-being in this region;

Fourth, as declared in the Southeast Asia Collective Defense Treaty, they are determined to prevent or counter by appropriate means any attempt in the treaty area to subvert their freedom or to destroy their sovereignty or territorial integrity.

SOUTHEAST ASIA COLLECTIVE DEFENSE TREATY OR MANILA PACT

ARTICLE I. The Parties undertake, as set forth in the Charter of the United Nations, to settle any international disputes in which they may be involved by peaceful means. . . .

ARTICLE II. In order more effectively to achieve the objectives of this Treaty, the Parties, separately and jointly, by means of continuous and effective self-help and mutual aid will maintain and develop their individual and collective capacity to resist armed attack and to prevent and counter subversive activities directed from without against their territorial integrity and political stability.

ARTICLE III. The Parties undertake to strengthen their free institutions and to cooperate with one another in the further development of economic measures, including technical assistance. . . .

ARTICLE IV. 1. Each Party recognizes that aggression by means of armed attack in the treaty area against any of the Parties or against any State or territory which the Parties by unanimous agreement may hereafter designate, would endanger its own peace and safety, and agrees that it will in that event act to meet the common danger in accordance with its constitutional processes. Measures taken under this paragraph shall be immediately reported to the Security Council of the United Nations.

2. If, in the opinion of any of the Parties, the inviolability or the integrity of the territory or the sovereignty or political independence of any Party in the treaty area or of any other State or territory to which the provisions of paragraph 1 of this Article from time to time apply is threatened in any way other than by armed attack or is affected or threatened by any fact or situation which might endanger the peace of the area, the Parties shall consult immediately in order to agree on the measures which should be taken for the common defense.

3. It is understood that no action on the territory of any State designated by unanimous agreement under paragraph 1 of this Article or on any territory so designated shall be taken except at the invitation or with the consent of the government concerned.

ARTICLE V. The Parties hereby establish a Council, on which each of them shall be represented, to consider matters concerning the implementation of this treaty. . . .

Understanding of the United States of America

The United States in executing the present Treaty does so with the understanding that its recognition of the effect of aggression and armed attack and its agreement with reference thereto in Article IV, paragraph 1, apply only to communist aggression but affirms that in the event of other aggression or armed attack it will consult under the provisions of Article IV, paragraph 2.

PROTOCOL TO THE SOUTHEAST ASIA COLLECTIVE DEFENSE TREATY

Designation of states and territory as to which provisions of Article IV and Article III are to be applicable:

The Parties to the Southeast Asia Collective Defense
Treaty unanimously designate for the purposes of Article
IV of the treaty the States of Cambodia and Laos and the
free territory under the jurisdiction of the State of Viet-
nam.

— 80 —

NINE-POWER AGREEMENT ON GERMANY AND EUROPEAN DEFENSE, OCTOBER 3 1954[1]

*By 1951 NATO had military headquarters in Paris and
a Supreme Commander in General Eisenhower; but it
lacked armed manpower. The United States advocated the
inclusion of German divisions in NATO's forces, but
France strongly objected. However, the United States
argued, a rearmed and sovereign Germany might be kept
from reverting to type within an organic European Defence Community in which France, Italy and the Benelux
states would have the dominant authority. When the
French Assembly rejected EDC on August 30, 1954,
Great Britain proposed that the Brussels Treaty Organization of which Britain, France and the Benelux countries
were members, be substituted for it. This proposal led to
agreement in London on a plan for associating the German Federal Republic fully with the defense of western
Europe within the controlling framework of an enlarged
Brussels Treaty organization, sometimes referred to as
Western European Union. The French were less impressed by the elaborate treaty guarantees that German
rearmament would be kept within bounds than by Great*

[1] From *Department of State Bulletin*, XXXI, No. 798 (Oct.
11, 1954), pp. 515-522.

Britain's pledge to maintain four divisions on the continent.

✓   ✓   ✓

I. GERMANY

The Governments of France, the United Kingdom and the United States declare that their policy is to end the Occupation régime in the Federal Republic as soon as possible, to revoke the Occupation Statute and to abolish the Allied High Commission. The Three Governments will continue to discharge certain responsibilities in Germany arising out of the international situation. . . .

II. BRUSSELS TREATY

The Brussels Treaty will be strengthened and extended to make it a more effective focus of European integration.

For this purpose the following arrangements have been agreed upon:

(a) The German Federal Republic and Italy will be invited to accede to the Treaty, suitably modified to emphasize the objective of European unity, and they have declared themselves ready to do so. The system of mutual automatic assistance in case of attack will thus be extended to the German Federal Republic and Italy.

(b) The structure of the Brussels Treaty will be reinforced. In particular the Consultative Council provided in the Treaty will become a Council with powers of decision.

(c) The activities of the Brussels Treaty Organization will be extended to include further important tasks as follows:

—The size and general characteristics of the German defence contribution will conform to the contribution fixed for EDC.

—The maximum defence contribution to NATO of all members of the Brussels Treaty Organization will be determined by a special agreement fixing levels which can only be increased by unanimous consent. . . .

IV. NATO

The powers present at the Conference which are members of NATO agreed to recommend at the next ministerial meeting of the North Atlantic Council that the Federal Republic of Germany should forthwith be invited to become a member.

They further agreed to recommend to NATO that its machinery be reinforced in the following respects:

(a) All forces of NATO countries stationed on the continent of Europe shall be placed under the authority of SACEUR with the exception of those which NATO has recognized or will recognize as suitable to remain under national command.

(b) Forces placed under SACEUR on the Continent shall be deployed in accordance with NATO strategy.

(c) The location of such forces shall be determined by SACEUR after consultation and agreement with the national authorities concerned. . . .

V. DECLARATION BY THE GERMAN FEDERAL GOVERNMENT AND JOINT DECLARATION BY THE GOVERNMENTS OF FRANCE, UNITED KINGDOM AND UNITED STATES OF AMERICA . . .

The German Federal Republic has agreed to conduct its policy in accordance with the principles of the Charter of the United Nations and accepts the obligations set forth in Article 2 of the Charter.

Upon her accession to the North Atlantic Treaty and the Brussels Treaty, the German Federal Republic declares that she will refrain from any action inconsistent with the strictly defensive character of the two treaties. In particular the German Federal Republic undertakes never to have recourse to force to achieve the reunification of Germany or the modification of the present boundaries of the German Federal Republic, and to resolve by peaceful means any disputes which may arise between the Federal Republic and other States.

The Governments of the United States, the United Kingdom and the French Republic . . . declare that

1. They consider the Government of the Federal Republic as the only German Government freely and legitimately constituted and therefore entitled to speak for Germany as the representative of the German people in international affairs.

2. In their relations with the Federal Republic they will

follow the principles set out in Article 2 of the United Nations Charter.

3. A peace settlement for the whole of Germany, freely negotiated between Germany and her former enemies, which should lay the foundation of a lasting peace, remains an essential aim of their policy. The final determination of the boundaries of Germany must await such a settlement.

4. The achievement through peaceful means of a fully free and unified Germany remains a fundamental goal of their policy.

5. The security and welfare of Berlin and the maintenance of the position of the Three Powers there are regarded by the Three Powers as essential elements of the peace of the free world in the present international situation. Accordingly they will maintain armed forces within the territory of Berlin as long as their responsibilities require it. They therefore reaffirm that they will treat any attack against Berlin from any quarter as an attack upon their forces and themselves.

6. They will regard as a threat to their own peace and safety any recourse to force which in violation of the principles of the United Nations Charter threatens the integrity and unity of the Atlantic alliance or its defensive purposes. In the event of any such action, the three Governments, for their part, will consider the offending government as having forfeited its rights to any guarantee and any military assistance provided for in the North Atlantic Treaty and its protocols. . . .

— 81 —

THE FORMOSA RESOLUTION, JANUARY 28, 1955 [1]

In December 1954, the United States government agreed to defend Nationalist China's Taiwan, or Formosa,

[1] *Department of State Bulletin*, XXXII, No. 815 (Feb. 7, 1955), p. 213.

and the Pescadores. On January 24 following, President Eisenhower asked Congress for authority to employ armed forces in actions "which might be necessary" to carry out the agreement. With only three opposing votes in each House, Congress gave the President plenary authority to do whatever was required to defend Formosa and the Pescadores. Since Mr. Eisenhower as Commander-in-Chief already had authority to take military action, it is probable that the main purpose of the resolution was to warn Communist China that neither the President nor Congress looked on the defense treaty with Chiang Kai-shek as merely ceremonial.

ʏ   ʏ   ʏ

. . . . Whereas certain territories in the West Pacific under the jurisdiction of the Republic of China are now under armed attack, and threats and declarations have been made and are being made by the Chinese Communists that such armed attack is in aid of and in preparation for armed attack on Formosa and the Pescadores, . . .

Whereas the President of the United States on January 6, 1955, submitted to the Senate for its advice and consent to ratification a Mutual Defense Treaty between the United States and the Republic of China. . . .

Therefore be it resolved by the Senate and House of Representatives of the United States in Congress assembled,

That the President of the United States be and he hereby is authorized to employ the Armed Forces of the United States as he deems necessary for the specific purpose of securing and protecting Formosa and the Pescadores against armed attack, this authority to include the securing and protection of such related positions and territories of that area now in friendly hands and the taking of such other measures as he judges to be required or appropriate in assuring the defense of Formosa and the Pescadores.

This resolution shall expire when the President shall determine that the peace and security of the area is reasonably assured by international conditions created by action of the United Nations or otherwise, and shall so report to the Congress.

EISENHOWER DOCTRINE: MIDDLE EAST, MARCH 9, 1957[1]

With the stated purpose of preventing Soviet aggression, President Eisenhower on January 5, 1957, asked Congress for authority to give assistance to any Middle East state or states requesting it, and to employ United States armed forces in the area as he judged necessary. Congress was not averse to voting an anti-Communist Manifesto, but before the Eisenhower Doctrine had been expressed in legislation nine weeks later, the Eisenhower-Dulles policy in the Middle East had been subjected to searching scrutiny in the Senate. In the end Congress did not "authorize" the President to employ armed forces, as it had in the Formosa resolution, but left the decision and entire responsibility to him. While the Act posted the Middle East against Soviet trespassing, it left the basic dilemmas of the area to be dealt with.

✓   ✓   ✓

Joint resolution to promote peace and stability in the Middle East.

Resolved by the Senate and House of Representatives of the United States of America in Congress assembled,

That the President be and hereby is authorized to co-operate with and assist any nation or group of nations in the general area of the Middle East desiring such assistance in the development of economic strength dedicated to the maintenance of national independence.

Section 2. The President is authorized to undertake, in

[1] From *The New York Times,* March 6, 1957. The resolution was signed on March 9.

the general area of the Middle East, military assistance programs with any nation or group of nations of that area desiring such assistance. Furthermore, the United States regards as vital to the national interest and world peace the preservation of the independence and integrity of the nations of the Middle East. To this end, if the President determines the necessity thereof, the United States is prepared to use armed forces to assist any such nation or group of such nations requesting assistance against armed aggression from any country controlled by international communism: Provided that such employment shall be consonant with the treaty obligations of the United States and with the Constitution of the United States.

Section 3. The President is hereby authorized to use during the balance of fiscal year 1957 for economic and military assistance under this joint resolution not to exceed $200,000,000 from any appropriation now available for carrying out the provisions of the Mutual Security Act of 1954, as amended. . . .

Section 4. The President should continue to furnish facilities and military assistance, under the provisions of applicable law and established policies, to the United Nations emergency force in the Middle East, with a view to maintaining the truce in that region.

Section 5. The President shall within the months of January and July of each year report to the Congress his actions hereunder.

Section 6. This Joint resolution shall expire when the President shall determine that the peace and security of the nations in the general area of the Middle East are reasonably assured by international conditions created by action of the United Nations or otherwise except that it may be terminated earlier by a concurrent resolution of the two houses of Congress.

VAN NOSTRAND ANVIL BOOKS already published